MW01616261

Counsel for the
Deceived

PHILIP G. SCHRAG

·

Counsel for the Deceived

Case Studies in Consumer Fraud

PANTHEON BOOKS

A Division of Random House, New York

Copyright © 1972 by Philip G. Schrag

All rights reserved under International and Pan-American Copyright
Conventions. Published in the United States by Pantheon Books, a division of Random House, Inc., New York, and simultaneously in Canada
by Random House of Canada Limited, Toronto.

Library of Congress Cataloging in Publication Data

Schrag, Philip, 1943– , Counsel for the deceived.

Includes bibliographical references.
1. Consumer protection—Law and legislation—New
York (City)   I. Title.

KFX2031.S35   343'.7471'07   70–39719   ISBN 0–394–47999–8

The names of all corporations and individuals except Department
of Consumer Affairs employees have been changed to conceal
their identities.

Manufactured in the United States of America
by the Colonial Press Inc., Clinton, Mass.

FIRST EDITION

FOR MOTHER AND DAD

Introduction

IN THEIR STUDIES of simpler societies around the world, anthropologists have told us of the functions of myth and abstraction in sustaining popular and uncritical faith in social systems. Our legal system could have benefited considerably if some of these anthropologists had stayed home and studied it. For precisely the same phenomena of myth and abstraction have persisted to make the legal system appear to be what it is not. Accordingly, lawyers and judges can maximize their parochial interests undeterred by external scrutiny, challenge, and reform.

The easy abstraction, for example, that if people have legal rights, they have justice, or the myth that citizens have access to and can use the legal system, were repeated so often and so authoritatively by the legal establishments that they became, until the early sixties, articles of faith to be intoned rather than propositions to be examined. Law students were told that this is a government of law, not of men, without the qualification that the thought is far more an ideal than a reality. Such a qualification might have focused the students' attention on ugly data and dismaying empirical studies. It might have taken them away from the preferred law school pattern of abstract digressions or "bread and butter" study by rote. The process of student acculturation to myth and abstraction was rigorous indeed in this shaping period of their careers.

The sixties was the decade when the law was forced to come down to earth. Laymen, particularly the poor and the young, forced the legal system to reveal its discriminatory, dilatory, costly, and often corrupt impact. That the challenges had to be as direct as the "sit-in" pointed to the level of stimulus required to change the law, although the majesty of the law is supposedly illuminated by less behavorial prods —such as principles of equity and justice. Certainly the handful of lawyers who took up cases in consumer, environment, housing, military, and other areas of primal legal challenge have strong grounds for repudiating the myths surrounding the legal system and documenting the raw realities about how it works and how it is being used.

Different questions need to be given prominence in an effort to genuinely appraise the faults which impede the administration of justice, and to propose needed remedies and reforms. A few suggestions: (1) To what extent does the monopoly of representation accorded lawyers contribute to or sustain arcane practices, costly hurdles, and biases which severely reduce the responsiveness of courts and regulatory agencies? (2) Why are most Americans effectively shut out of the formal legal system in resolving disputes with firms, institutions, and governments? (3) What outside forces cause the aggrieved to feel intimidated by the legal system—even when the law is "on their side"? (4) Just what do legal rights mean without the easy availability of legal representation and remedies? (5) What defense mechanisms (such as the corporate shell) does the law support which eliminate the value of any judgment or decision beyond technical recognition of rights? (6) How is the law itself being used as an instrument for oppression or retardation? (7) Who defines what is violent or fraudulent as far as the practical attention given to these activities by law enforcement? (8) What determines the deployment of the legal profession so that the respective needs for justice and foresight by various segments of our society become the least relevant consideration? (9) Can the legal system as presently defined be expanded into less formal and more accessible institutions to permit conflict resolution without requiring the aggrieved to lose more than is gained in time, money, and other attendant risks? (10) How can accountability be built into large commercial and governmental institutions and backed up by the law?

Many of these questions are stimulated most concretely by Philip G. Schrag as he describes the consumer abuse cases he handled as a young lawyer with the NAACP Legal Defense Fund and the New York City Department of Consumer Affairs led by Bess Myerson. Several lawyer-writers before Schrag have documented the abuses in the law writ large; very few, however, have engaged in the meticulous firsthand description of cases as they happened—beginning with the interaction between commerce and consumer then winding down the tortuous path of the law and the courts. In some ways, this book is an autobiography of Schrag's career over the past four years since his graduation from Yale Law School. It is a rare combination of observation, reflection, and confession—the kind of narrative-analysis which compels one to recommend it highly to all first-year law students. They will come of age rapidly after reading this compressed record of disillusionment with the wretched practices of much of the judicial system. Perhaps most important, they will learn a new way of thinking—starting from empirical observation and recorded data about problems affecting millions of people and then moving on to levels of legal abstraction meaningfully rooted in reality.

Schrag kept voluminous records of his cases and later interviewed the Department's lawyers at length. The details presented reflect the value of such sources over even the best of memories. He depicts the human consequences for consumers deceived by the "holder in due course" doctrine, "sewer service" practice, unconscionable procedural delays

to erode the will and resources of the plaintiff, jockeying for
the "right" judges by corporate defendants, the absence of
effective sanctions in the pre-trial and post-judgment phases,
the flexibility of corporate shells and their counsel to evade
even being brought to the judicial forum and the insulation
of "respectable" corporations, such as banks and finance
companies, that support or supply the less savory operators,
but escape accountability, liability, or exposure of their role.
Regarding the latter situation, Schrag concludes one case description of an outrageously fraudulent sales scheme of burglar alarms this way:

> But the Foolproof case illustrates another way in which
> major corporations help gyp the American public—not direct-
> ly, not visibly, but from behind the scenes, by extending mu-
> tually profitable lifelines to companies whose business prac-
> tices they do not wish to know very much about. Foolproof's
> protectors included a major department store, five banks (in-
> cluding one enormous bank), a prestigious law firm, one of
> whose partners became a . . . director [of its parent corpora-
> tion], an underwriting company, and a public relations secu-
> rities firm. The company also had a way to generate a tele-
> phone call from City Hall.

Schrag aptly underscores how frequently consumers don't
know they are being gypped or don't know how to complain.
Those that realize they have a complaint, particularly
among the low income areas of New York City, despair from
doing so because they believe no one in officialdom will listen
and nothing will be done. He illustrates the enormous time
and manpower which a single case can absorb and even after
a successful adjudication, the deterrent effect on others never
took hold. The reader may be sensitive, at the book's end, to
Schrag's feeling of utter frustration with his four-year effort
as counsel for the deceived. He did manage to produce a few
ripples of justice in an ocean of fraud and commercial chi-
canery, but achieved little, if anything, he felt, of enduring
significance and quantitative change for consumer justice.
Even though the new New York City Consumer Protection

Act, which he drafted and lobbied, provided for powers of injunction and mass restitutions of monies bilked from consumers, Schrag feared that the strategies, resources, and numbers of potential corporate defendants would be repeatedly decisive.

It is too early to despair. The cost-benefit of greatly increased enforcement resources, under effectively drafted consumer laws, has not been shown to be futile. Indeed, it has not been tried. We are a nation, after all, which in 1970 devoted more public funds to building one C-5-A cargo plane than to the budget ($125 million) of the entire federal court system. After decades of no enforcement, it will take more than a few months to build a momentum that communicates its determination to deter corporate or business crime—both blue-chip and what the author calls the harder core "commercial underworld." In order to achieve this redirection away from fraudulent practices, the law must override the buffers of corporatism, so well recounted in this volume, and reach the individuals who direct these operations. Only a more refined and focused sense of outrage by larger numbers of consumers will create the democratic pressures which politicians, administrators, and judges cannot ignore. To give such widening and proper outrage over consumer exploitations a cutting edge is the mission of lawyers and other professionals who are staffing local, state, and federal consumer protection agencies and public interest law groups around the country. At the beginnings of any movement for greater justice, it is easy to generalize from the early stumblings that the crimes are substantially beyond the limits of effective legal action. To deny this conclusion is not to fail to recognize that much work needs to be done outside formal regulatory and adjudicatory institutions—in the media, in consumer organizations, in the electoral and legislative system, in the professions, in the ethical whistleblowing arena, and in the use of many other levers of change.

In his concluding chapter, Schrag discusses various enforcement models in terms of strengths and weaknesses. He describes the needed development of neighborhood consumer tribunals that would be "open during the evening, or on weekends, so that people who work need not have to choose between justice and their jobs." It is clear from his words that Schrag is still searching for workable models. In his present position as Associate Professor of Law at Columbia University, he will have more time to reflect on his experience. Earlier than many of his contemporaries, Schrag saw the gravity of the epidemic of consumer injustice not only afflicting the poor with special viciousness, but also distorting the entire economic system.

The manipulation by corporations of what economists call the "consumption function" has attained an entrenchment which makes it a major allocator of resources and a major distributor of hazards to the consumer's health and safety. During the past decade exposures in the auto, pharmaceutical, pesticide, food, and pollution industries have given the consumer movement dimensions of importance that go to the nucleus of the society's power structure and its directions for the future. The direct and indirect quality and quantity of the consumption function is more the test of the society's standard of living than the "production function" which has received historically far greater attention—particularly in an economy of wealth that has little difficulty anymore in merely producing. *What* is produced, to *whom* it is distributed, and at what *cost* inside and outside the market are consumption questions. Together with widespread price-fixing and administered pricing, a host of anti-competitive practices have helped block the timely feedback from the consumer pressure point on both economic and safety grounds. At stake are tens of billions of dollars in waste, fraud, excess profits, and by-product costs every year. The call one hears increasingly for a system to measure better the quality of the economy, not just the gross national product, mirrors a growing awareness that our trillion-dollar-plus annual economic output is failing to treat many pressing domestic deprivations—such as poverty, housing, public services—formerly thought to be responsive to economic growth. And it is also creating new problems—more pollution, more occupational diseases, more draining bureaucracies, more transportation and court congestion—without reallocating resources.

Mr. Schrag's localized case studies are only among the more apparent symptoms of a malaise spreading itself on the consumer in an economy dominated by corporate giants which have perfected ways, often with the complicity of indentured government (such as the oil import quotas' $6 billion annual consumer overcharge), to derivatively bilk consumers far removed from them in time and space. The consumer movement must grapple with this closed enterprise system and its controlled market if the fruits of labor are not to be dissipated by consumers spending for needlessly imposed costs or ingeniously contrived frauds.

RALPH NADER

Preface

FOR FIFTEEN MONTHS, between April 1970 and July 1971, I
directed the newly created Law Enforcement Division of the
New York City Department of Consumer Affairs. I had an
opportunity to observe how companies of all types and sizes
abuse their consumers, to compare the "reputable" supermarkets whose advertised specials are somehow never available with the fly-by-night con men whose deliberate swindles
cause financially stable families to become impoverished in a
matter of days. In hundreds of hours of conversation with
businessmen and buyers, I came to appreciate the simple
truth of Woody Guthrie's line: "Well it's through this world
I've rambled/I've seen lots of funny men/Some rob you with
a six-gun/Some with a fountain pen."

But consumer fraud is only the subsidiary theme of this
volume. Primarily, this is a book about government, about
the experiences of young lawyers who had enough faith in
the administrative process to become part of it. They found
that despite their pioneering spirit and their readiness to
make new precedents, despite their willingness to work whatever hours were required, despite even new legislation to arm
them with the tools they needed, their trust in the effective-

ness of government was diffused by contact with a legal system capable of exhausting the most dedicated advocates by permitting endless delay. Nor could they substantially help consumers even when they were able to overcome systemic delay and obtain decisions from courts, for the judges they encountered were anything but friendly to their position.

Agencies have been known to react to similar sets of affairs by going to sleep. Perhaps the same fate will eventually befall the Department of Consumer Affairs. But in the short run, at least, the lawyers' reaction was to fight back by inventing new modes of official behavior which did not depend upon use of the legal and judicial systems. This pattern may become increasingly prevalent now that activists—both lawyers and laymen—are rediscovering the importance of state and local government and are competing for work in their agencies.

This book documents some of the frauds we encountered, the procedural system we were expected to use to fight those frauds, and the devices we adopted when we saw that the normal processes were not adequate. It is a history of what happens at the usually invisible lowest layer of government, for it reveals the types of activity and decision-making by agency staff that ultimately determine many apparently top-level administrative actions. What really happened is rarely told by the innocuous press release or newspaper story, and even the memoirs of government officials are generally biased by the fact that the officials who write memoirs have usually occupied positions at the highest rungs of government; they themselves have not known how their administrations functioned, at their lowest level, day by day.

Although the events here reported could not have taken place without Commissioner Bess Myerson, this is not a book *about* Bess Myerson. It is instead a study of the hundreds of minute decisions that in the aggregate determine the course and test the effectiveness of a government agency.

Contents

Counsel for the Deceived

1 · How Laws Are Passed

WHEN I GRADUATED from law school in 1967, I went to work for the NAACP Legal Defense and Educational Fund. My first client was the victim of a classic consumer fraud, and he epitomized the problem of consumer protection in the late 1960's: although the rights of consumers were being rapidly expanded, enforcement of those rights was almost non-existent.

Frank Allen was a Negro in his twenties. He had a tenth-grade education, lived in a New York City housing project, and earned about $5,000 a year. His wife also worked; she earned a little less than that. In March 1966, at the suggestion of a friend of the Allens, a door-to-door salesman named Richard had visited the Allens in their apartment, and had made an offer that seemed appealing. Richard represented Super Fine Furniture, a large Harlem store, in business for 133 years. For less than $20 a week, he would provide them with all the food they and their four-year-old daughter needed, so they would not have to whittle away their budget at grocery stores or supermarkets. He showed them a long list of the meats that he would supply, and, "just to see how this would work to save money for you," he made up a list of the groceries they usually bought, which he would also supply. "This is a budget savings plan," he said. "We buy in bulk, and so we can pass the savings on to you. You will find this plan much cheaper than buying food in the stores. And all our food is the highest quality, Grade A." He noted that the Allens would still have to buy milk and fresh vegetables in the store, but that his plan would supply everything else they needed. "This food will be delivered monthly," he said, "and you will need some place to store it, so I will also provide you with a fine freezer, which will be less than $8 a week, but the savings on the food will be so great that the freezer pays for itself and is essentially free."

Mr. and Mrs. Allen always had trouble with their budget and were constantly in debt, so they were inclined to accept. Richard assured them that they could cancel the whole deal after four months, simply by not reordering food at that time. So Mr. and Mrs. Allen signed the contract. They did not read it first because they could see that it was written in legalistic language they could not understand; and in any event, Richard seemed like an honest fellow, represented one of the largest Harlem stores, and had come recommended by their friend. (Mr. Allen later found out that his friend had signed up for a food plan a few days before, and Richard had given him a $25 discount for recommending a friend who would also sign a contract.)

A week later, a great volume of food arrived, along with a freezer. The food was not the high quality Mr. Allen expected, but it was tolerable. The quantity, however, was so small that the food ran out long before the four months ended; the Allens had to buy as much from stores in the final weeks of the period as they did before they started the plan.

A week after the food and freezer came, Mr. Allen received two coupon books—one for the food and one for the freezer—from Regal Finance Co. One set of coupons required him to pay $30.22 a month; the other required him to pay $74.83 per month. Mr. Allen looked at the books, saw that he did not have to make his first payment for about four weeks, and threw the books—along with the accompanying forms—into a drawer until the first payments were due. (At this point, he wasn't sure whether the food supply would last or not.)

After grumbling for four months, but making all payments on time, Mr. Allen called Richard at a number the salesman had left and told him that he was not reordering because he was dissatisfied with the inadequate quantity of food supplied. "You can pick up the freezer any time," he said. "Oh no," said Richard, "you can cancel the food, but you may not cancel payments on the freezer. Sorry, you've signed a written contract to buy it by paying $30.22 a month for three years. Look at your copy of the contract."

Mr. Allen looked at the contract and saw for the first time that he had agreed in writing, not to rent a freezer, but to buy one at a price of $1,087 over three years. He was shocked by the price because he had never heard of a freezer costing more than three or four hundred dollars. "I'm going to talk to a lawyer," he told Richard. "Don't do that," said Richard. "I'll straighten this out and call you back." He never did.

Mr. Allen went to see his union's lawyer, who told him that contracts were binding and that once he signed, there was nothing he could do. "Besides," said the lawyer, "it appears that a credit company bought your contract; and if you don't keep up your payments, they'll garnishee your wages and you may be fired."

Mr. Allen kept up his payments for fourteen months, becoming angrier with each payment. Finally he went to the Legal Aid Society, which referred him to me.

Mr. Allen was one of millions of people bilked every year by false advertising or fast-talking salesmen. Although estimates of the dollar volume of consumer fraud are risky, home improvement swindles alone are said to cost Americans over a billion dollars a year, counterfeit branding of merchandise two billion, and medical quackery another billion.[1] The New York City Department of Consumer Affairs receives 20,000 complaints a year, almost all of them justified; at that rate, there would be half a million complaints nationwide. But it is obvious that that figure grossly understates the volume of abuse, because only a very small minority—I would guess fewer than 1%—of the victims of consumer fraud complain to a government agency. The most frequent and serious complaints of fraud usually involve mail orders, furniture, appliances, health and reducing products, correspondence courses, money-making schemes or door-to-door sales of a variety of products, from encyclopedias and magazine subscriptions to pots and pans.

From one perspective, Mr. Allen and the thousands like him were fortunate: the law theoretically offered them redress. If the legal system worked as intended, Mr. Allen could have a court declare the contract invalid because of the salesman's false promise about the sufficiency of the food, either in a suit brought by Mr. Allen against the store and finance company, or in a suit by the finance company against him, provoked by his failure to send it any more payments.

In such a suit, it was true, Mr. Allen would have had to overcome a serious obstacle: the finance company would claim to be a "holder in due course." [2] Regal Finance had printed the contract form, which it had supplied to Super Fine Furniture. Because every year it bought from Super Fine (and from other slum furniture stores) the right to collect monthly payments from thousands of consumers who signed such forms, it had included in the form a crucial fine-print clause. That clause—one of several under which Mr. Allen had signed his name—said that the buyer of the merchandise agreed to waive all his rights in the event that the seller (Super Fine) sold the contract to a finance company. In other words, although the law gave Mr. Allen the right not to pay *the store* if it cheated him, it permitted him to sign away that right as against a finance company which bought contracts from the store. Under the principle of the holder in due course, Mr. Allen would have to pay the finance company even if the freezer had arrived ruined, or even if the store had never delivered it.

However, the use of this device to undermine consumer rights was coming under sharp attack. Two or three state legislatures forbade it during the late 1960's, and occasionally a court would find an excuse not to apply the doctrine. Mr. Allen, therefore, had at least a fighting chance—in theory.

But as a practical matter, consumers such as Mr. Allen had almost no protection, for two reasons. First, more important than the consumer's right to get his money back is his right not to be cheated in the first place, and neither the public agencies charged with guarding this right nor the remedies administered by courts in consumer litigation were effective in deterring the practice of consumer fraud. Mr. Allen might win his own case, return his freezer, and get his money back, but that would hardly stop Super Fine and its salesmen from making similar misrepresentations to dozens of other consumers who would grudgingly pay an unjust debt rather than fight an exhausting court battle. Second, the law would at best return to Mr. Allen the money he had paid; it would not compensate him for the time he had to invest in interviews with his lawyer, required pre-trial appearances in the offices of the store's or finance company's attorneys, or court appearances. Nor would it pay his attorney for the time spent locating, interviewing, and preparing witnesses, or preparing hundreds of pages of affidavits and briefs which might be necessary to win the case.

The Federal Trade Commission (FTC) is the government agency primarily entrusted with the task of preventing consumer fraud. But some time during the 1960's, the FTC virtually ground to a halt as a result of inadequate funding, understaffing, conservative interpretations of its power, lack of public support, overbureaucratization, and the absence of any real sense of mission.

For example, in 1968 the FTC, with jurisdiction over consumer fraud in interstate commerce anywhere in the nation, issued only 45 complaints against deceptive practices, of which all but 16 were consented to.[3] It referred only 3 such cases to the Department of Justice for enforcement proceedings.[4] Only one out of 125 avowed applications for a complaint—pre-screened for apparent relevance and appropriate jurisdiction—resulted in formal FTC action.[5] Furthermore, when the commission did act, it did so at an impossibly slow pace. The average case took 4.37 years from the "investigation" phase (which might follow a complaint by several months) to the issuance of a cease and desist order,[6] and since that order can be appealed, cases have been known to take twenty years or more.[7] Meanwhile, the company did not have to change its practices, and it was routine for firms to complete their advertising and promotional campaigns years before the FTC concluded that the practices were deceptive and should not be used in the future.

Even when the Commission acted promptly, it believed itself to lack legislative authority to get money back for defrauded consumers, so its strongest penalty was merely an order to a company to refrain from future fraud, a gentle pat on the wrist.

The FTC's low level of activity was explained by observers to result in good measure from its recruitment and personnel practices, and the attitudes of the lawyers it hired. Influential Congressmen, particularly Southern Democrats, determined many staff appointments and promotions; "the atmosphere of the agency was like a Southern county courthouse." [8] Many young applicants were accepted by the commission not because of their grades or extracurricular activities, but because of "old school ties, regional background, or a political endorsement," [9] or because of selection by one of the Bureau Chiefs who preferred "attorneys who will not underscore their mediocrity or disturb the work patterns of the bureau." [10] One senior staff member of the FTC admitted that "he preferred to hire older men—who had been out in the world for ten years or so and had come to appreciate that they were not going to make much of a mark—because they tended to be loyal and remain with the FTC." [11]

Mr. Allen and other consumers could expect little more protection from state consumer protection agencies. In fact,

Mr. Allen had gone to the Office of the New York State Attorney General before he came to me; an Assistant Attorney General had called Regal Finance on his behalf, but when Regal refused to refund any money, he told Mr. Allen there was nothing he could do. Across the country, state consumer agencies and bureaus were havens for political hacks. They had few powers and requested no more; they saw themselves as mediation services for those few who complained, rather than law enforcement agencies established to stop the exploitation of buyers.[12]

In the absence of a government agency willing to be the consumer's advocate, there was little hope of frightening a company into adopting honest selling techniques. Consumers had great difficulty finding legal counsel of any sort. Mr. Allen's union lawyer had turned him down because without substantial compensation—which Mr. Allen was unable to pay—he could not afford to spend a large amount of time fighting the case. The Legal Aid Society had turned him down because his total family income was in the range of $10,000, above the society's eligibility limits.[13] I could accept his case only because the NAACP Legal Defense Fund was supported by private contributions to enable it to participate in selected "test" litigation, but few other lawyers were so fortunate, and I couldn't accept more than about half a dozen cases a year.

Even when a consumer could obtain an attorney, the attorney could do little about the deceptive practice involved. The law did not authorize lawsuits (except by the government agencies, which rarely used the power) to enjoin consumer frauds. Suits for treble or punitive damages against companies engaging in deception might, if successful, have a deterrent effect, but scant precedent existed for that course of action either.

Finally, consumers who did not consult attorneys were as good as lost. Thousands of them were cheated every year. Those who had bought for cash had no recourse at all. Those who purchased on credit usually stopped paying in protest.

The store or finance company in question would send them a series of increasingly nasty dunning letters, telephone their employers to increase the pressure, and then bring suits for collection. In many cases, the consumers who were sued never learned of that fact until they lost the cases and their wages were garnisheed. Although the law requires that people be notified at the outset of suits against them, process servers charged with the job of providing notice frequently found it more convenient to tear up the summonses and file perjured affidavits that they had given them to the defendants.[14] Those defendants, particularly poor defendants, who actually received notice of a lawsuit usually did not appear in court to defend the cases. Inability to obtain time off from work, distance from the courthouse, the requirement of multiple appearances, the incomprehensibility of the summons forms, complex procedure, and fear of "the law" combined to make the rate of judgments by default in consumer credit cases awesomely high—perhaps 90% nationally and over 96% in some metropolitan areas, such as New York. One study of over a thousand consumer cases in Detroit, Chicago, and New York revealed that trials had occurred in only seven of them.[15]

Since test litigation was my job, Mr. Allen's case became a challenge to what seemed the most serious problem of consumer protection—the lack of remedies that would deter. We asked $50,000 in punitive damages against the store and the finance company for misleading dozens of freezer purchasers pursuant to a vicious pattern of conduct aimed at the buying public. I have elsewhere recounted at some length a month-by-month history of the lawsuit.[16] In brief, hundreds of man-hours were expended on both sides. Over the course of months, Regal's attorneys exercised their right to pre-trial cross-examination of the Allens for several days, then rigidly resisted our attempts to obtain corresponding investigation of the companies' practices. Motions and counter-motions proliferated; delays built on delays; pounds of paper were filed with the court; affidavits and briefs pertaining to the most trivial points of procedure flew back and forth among the lawyers working on the case. The months became years; the likelihood that the court would ever consider the substance of the case (whether the Allens were cheated and whether, if so, they could collect punitive damages) became ever dimmer.

Meanwhile Ralph Nader persuaded politicians that consumer protection could be a popular issue. Legislation was written, and much of it was passed. The newspapers talked of the age of the consumer. But the reforms were incomplete, and most of the new laws struck off in tangential directions. Legislators gave little attention to strengthening enforcement of existing prohibitions against deception in the sale of goods or services.

For most of the decade, for example, the members of Congress who were concerned with consumer protection pressed single-mindedly for enactment of the Truth-in-Lending law, which they achieved in the middle of 1968. The new law required contract forms to state the true annual interest rate which the buyer would be charged. It therefore added to preprinted forms yet another standard item which few consumers, particularly poor consumers, would read, and which, even if read, would probably not affect the decision to buy. It did a man little good to know that he was being charged, say, 18% a year, the maximum interest permitted by his state's law, if all other stores that would give him credit also charged 18% a year. Also, many stores and door-to-door salesmen catering to low-income buyers found an easy way to understate the true interest rate. Since state laws set ceilings on interest rates but did not regulate cash prices, and since these stores sold only for credit and never for cash, the stores assigned their wares artificial cash prices which were lower than the cost to the consumer by exactly the maximum lawful interest rate. Finally, the Truth-in-Lending law left merchants free to offer descriptions of the qualities of goods and services that were as false as they had been in the past.

Congress also held hearings on—but never passed—a proposed federal law to give door-to-door buyers the right to cancel their contracts within two days after signing them.[17] While this law would have helped some victims of high-pressure sales talk, it would not have been of much assistance to deceived consumers, who generally do not discover the deception at least until the goods are delivered, and usually not until weeks or months later. The Allens, for example, could not have known that the food delivered to their house would not last four months until the first two of those months had passed. Several states did pass "cooling-off period" laws, but as usual, insufficient attention was paid to enforcement procedures. Merchants routinely claimed that they had not received the notices of cancellation which the consumers mailed, and door-to-door salesmen back-dated contract forms so that it would appear, to a person looking at the contracts and at cancellation notices mailed on the actual day of signing, that the two or three days allowed by law for cancellation had run by the time the consumers' regrets matured.

Sharp criticism of the holder in due course doctrine led a few states to enact reforms to preserve buyers' rights against banks and finance companies, but except in Massachusetts, these new laws left enormous loopholes. They prohibited fine-print waiver clauses in installment *contracts,* but said nothing about such clauses in revolving charge account agreements. Soon, merchants began discarding their contract forms and signing their customers up for revolving charges. More important, the banks distributed millions of Master Charge and BankAmericard credit cards, many of them unsolicited, to consumers in all economic brackets, and authorized thousands of stores, including ghetto stores and even door-to-door salesmen, to accept them. The fine-print agreements mailed to buyers with the cards provided that the buyers waived against the banks their right to withhold payment because of a dispute with a seller. To agree to this condition, the buyers did not even have to sign the agreement; they merely had to use the card to make a purchase.

Finally, there occurred during this period the first stirrings of judicial concern over the fairness of the price in installment contracts. In a handful of cases, where sellers had marked goods up by more than 200%, courts refused to permit creditors to collect all the money that the contracts provided for, even though the buyers did not claim to have been lied to or misled.[18] But this newly developing doctrine of "the unconscionability of the price" only deepened the irony of the consumer's plight. It doubled or tripled the number of persons who had legal rights on paper, but practically no way to enforce them. Those few cases in which trials occurred were tributes to the patient efforts of a few dedicated legal aid or private attorneys who had taken special interest in particular clients or issues, and were willing to subsidize a consumer-litigant by devoting thousands of dollars worth of legal time to the defense of a three-hundred-dollar claim.

Those few trials also represented the unusual case in which the adversary system somehow failed to operate; for some reason, the sellers' attorneys did not manage to obscure the issues or indefinitely postpone resolution of the conflict. Mr. Allen's case, on the other hand, was interminable. At every stage, the lawyers for Super Fine Furniture and Regal Finance employed obstructive tactics to derail the case. Telephone calls were not returned. Witnesses failed to appear for scheduled examinations. Finally, for reasons unassociated with the Allen case, Super Fine went bankrupt, which prevented any resolution of the essential issue—a consumer's right to punitive damages; no store existed to defend the claim or pay any damages that might be awarded. Four years after the hike, the Allen case was settled at the line of scrimmage. Mr. Allen got no money back, but didn't have to make any more payments.

The Allen lawsuit was typical of my efforts to entice courts, through test litigation, to provide consumers with strengthened remedies; the strategy miscarried because few cases ever reached the "test" stage. As I became ever more entangled in the obstacles which could be erected within the system, I began to wonder whether it wouldn't make more sense to approach consumer law enforcement from an entirely different direction, by building a powerful and aggressive administrative agency, one that was capable even of overkill in the consumer's behalf, in order to redress the balance between the deceiving seller and the deceived buyer. Meanwhile, late in 1968, the New York City Council reacted to the popular wave of consumerism by creating a city Department of Consumer Affairs,[19] and a series of events began to occur which would give me the opportunity to test in practice whether, under the best of circumstances, government could really protect consumers from fraud and deception.

My brief career in government began because a law school classmate, a former fellow editor of the *Yale Law Journal*, was at that time working as a Special Assistant to Mayor John Lindsay, and consumer affairs happened to be among his areas of responsibility. Since he knew that I was active in the field, he called me to ask what the newly created agency should do. I told him that although I had some ideas about the matter, they would take a great deal of time and energy to implement. I then offered to devote that time and energy, provided that he arranged to have me appointed either Commissioner of Consumer Affairs or Chairman of the Department's statutorily established Advisory Council.

He explained that the administration really didn't approve of Commissioners under the age of thirty, but he did arrange the Chairmanship for me. I then began to build the kind of agency that I thought could make a difference.

All the City Council had done was to amalgamate the city's Department of Markets (Weights and Measures) with its Department of Licenses (which authorized fee-paying non-felons to operate cabarets, sidewalk cafés, miniature golf courses, and 102 other such sensitive industries). Although the Department's licensing jurisdiction did cover a few occupations in which licensing might actually be a useful tool of consumer protection—home improvement contractors, used car dealers, and employment agencies—the staffing and jurisdiction of the Department were not well geared to deterring and punishing consumer fraud generally. The City Council had merely given old agencies a new name, an advisory council, and, importantly, subpoena power.

It appeared to me that the agency needed a new law, a vigorous staff, and a tough image. I started with the law; the Advisory Council stole from other states and laws the best provisions we could find, added a few ideas of our own, and ended up with the toughest consumer protection bill we could imagine.

The bill we drafted forbade all deception whatsoever in the sale of consumer goods or services, in the extension of consumer credit, or the collection of consumer debts. We excluded all references to the seller's intent; a merchant would violate the law if his statement or advertisement had the "capacity, tendency or effect" of misleading consumers. Furthermore, we specifically provided that it would not be necessary to show that consumers were actually injured. We included a prohibition on the deceptive use of "exaggeration, innuendo or ambiguity as to a material fact or failure to state a material fact."

Taking our cue from the court cases that had reviewed the price of merchandise, we outlawed any "unconscionable" practices as well, and we gave the Commissioner of Consumer Affairs the power to issue regulations, without prior public hearing, defining types of practices as deceptive or unconscionable and therefore prohibited by the statute.

Of course, the section I cared most about concerned enforcement powers. We gave the Commissioner the power to seek a choice of four penalties in the courts—a civil fine of $50 to $350 for "accidental" violations;[20] $500 or $1,000 fines for "knowing" violations; injunctions (court orders to stop a particular practice), including preliminary injunctions and temporary restraining orders; and what we informally dubbed, for lack of a better term, "mass restitution." Under the mass restitution provision, the Commissioner could, where he found "multiple" violations, apply for a court order creating an escrow account of all the money "received as a result of such violations," which would be paid over by the Department "to any and all persons who purchased the goods or services during the period of violation . . . in a transaction involving the prohibited acts or practices." The escrow account would be enlarged to include also "any costs incurred by such claimants in making and pursuing their complaints," so that consumers would be made whole, if at all possible. Finally, the Department of Consumer Affairs, in such an action, would recover its costs of investigation from the defendant and also keep all the money in the escrow accounts which was unclaimed by consumers within one year after the Department publicized the accounts' existence in a manner approved by the court. The theory was that both consumers and the Department would never lose by investigating and suing a guilty company—both would recover their gross expenditures.

We deliberately required the agency to go to court to obtain penalties or remedies, rather than authorizing it to issue administrative penalties subject to court review. Legally, to enable it to issue cease and desist orders, we would have had to create not only a new investigative staff, but a separate, neutral staff of hearing officers as well. Furthermore, although an administrative procedure would seem to expedite cases compared to the slow pace of most litigation, stays pending appeal of administrative orders are granted by courts almost routinely, so that the two-step procedure—administrative hearing and judicial review—was likely, in important cases, to take longer than litigation. Finally, we had some doubt as to whether the City Council would pass a bill authorizing the agency itself to order remedies, particularly the important, drastic remedy of mass restitution.

Just as we finished drafting, the first Commissioner of Consumer Affairs, Gerard Weisberg, was appointed to the bench, and the Mayor chose Bess Myerson to succeed him. It is generally supposed that his motives were primarily political; he was up for re-election in a matter of months, and many of the city's Jews had defected from his camp during the school decentralization controversy. The appointment of a female Jewish television celebrity—a former Miss America —was a brilliant political move;[21] by accident or design it was also the best merit appointment he could have made. Not only was Commissioner Myerson quick to learn the field (including the legal aspects of consumer protection) and receptive to virtually all staff proposals, but her fame and charisma enabled her to win crucial battles with heads of other city agencies and to get almost any story about consumer fraud into the newspapers.

The Advisory Council presented its draft bill to Commissioner Myerson the day she was sworn in, early in March 1969, and she made its passage the primary goal of her first year in office. She immediately changed its name from the Unfair Trade Practices Act to the Consumer Protection Law, on the undoubtedly correct theory that a sexier title would aid enactment.

To a student for whom Congress is a model legislature, the New York City Council is a strange body. Relative to the Mayor, in theory, the council is very powerful; it can even, by simple majority vote, amend the City Charter. But by tradition, most of the thirty-seven part-time City Councilmen spend a majority of their spare hours performing services for individual constituents rather than working on legislation. They have never voted to give themselves staffs or private offices, and, except for one or two occasions a year when, on major issues, the council leadership drafts its own proposals, they are content to let the Mayor run the city and draft the legislation they enact. Such legislative power as the council chooses to exercise is delegated to one man—the majority leader. He has a staff assistant[22] and a City Hall office; he determines when and if committees will hold hearings and recommend legislation; he decides what will pass and what will not. Generally, if he permits a hearing on a bill, it will be brought to the floor and will pass with few dissenting votes; it would not be economical to take up the time of Councilmen holding hearings on bills not destined to pass. He works

closely with the Mayor's staff; amendments to bills are negotiated between him and the Mayor's people, rather than debated and contested in committee or on the floor of the council. Naturally, when we had drafted our bill and cleared it
through the city's Law Department, Commissioner Myerson
and I went to see the majority leader.

In a meeting in his office, he took the bill, heard our ex-
planation, and promised to call us. We didn't hear from him
for some time, so we feared the bill was dead. Commissioner
Myerson then began a long campaign of becoming the
squeaking wheel. For months, she wrote to him, she called
him, she visited him. Finally, he told her that bills only
passed the council when there was public pressure for them,
so the department's staff and the Advisory Council began to
manufacture some pressure—the usual letters, telegrams,
phone calls—all to the majority leader, who wanted to see
pressure, none to the other thirty-six Councilmen. At every
speaking engagement, Commissioner Myerson circulated a
petition for the bill among her audience, so that we were able
to present the majority leader with several thousand signa-
tures urging passage of the bill. Finally, after this game continued for several more months, the majority leader informed
us that one of the committees would hold a hearing on the
bill.

Two days before the hearing, the serious opposition mate-
rialized. Arthur Byers, a partner in a prestigious law firm
representing the trade association of major New York department stores, came to see me to express the association's opposition to the uncompromising text of the bill. He implied that
he would have the bill killed or amended if we did not agree
to certain amendments on which he insisted.

"Under this bill," said Byers, "there would be serious
penalties for violations of the Commissioner's regulations, but
it's impossible to comply with regulations."

"Why is it impossible?" I asked.

"For example," he said, "the Federal Trade Commission
says an advertisement for television sets which lists only the

diagonal screen measurement must identify the measurement as being diagonal. There are dozens of regulations like that. The girls who write advertising copy can't possibly remember all those regulations. Every now and then, they forget, but the omission doesn't hurt anyone. It's just a technical thing. We shouldn't be punished for it."

"Why can't they remember all the regulations?"

"That's the kind of help you get nowadays."

"But can't you hire some supervisor who knows all the regulations to look over all the ads?"

"You don't realize how many ads a big department store places every day," he told me. "It would cost a lot of money to increase supervision over copy just to comply with all of the technical regulations. The costs would be passed on to customers in the form of higher prices. You wouldn't want that, would you?"

It seemed to me I would. "That's pretty important," I said. "Saying that a set is twenty-one inches, when its width is only nineteen inches, misleads the customer unless the advertiser says he's talking about the diagonal."

"I don't mind making an adjustment if the consumer is really misled," said Byers. "But under this bill, you can punish a store even if no one is injured. Let's say that a store is selling chairs, and it puts up a big sign saying 'fire sale' even though there hasn't been a fire. And let's say it charges its customers $75 for chairs that are actually worth $75. Why should it be penalized if no one is injured? The sign may not be 100% true, but it doesn't make any difference."

"Then why do they put it up?" I asked.

"They sell more chairs that way," he said.

After about an hour of this, he asked me in what room of the Department's office the hearing would be held.

I was puzzled. "It's not being held at the Department," I said. "It's at the City Council."

"You mean this isn't a hearing to determine if the Commissioner should sponsor the bill?" he asked, visibly upset. "The council has scheduled a hearing?"

Someone, either Byers or the officers of his client, had been asleep at the switch. The reason we had gotten as far as we had was that the opposition hadn't done anything to stop us. And now it was really too late; the press had been informed of the hearing, and its cancellation would embarrass the council. Also, the hearing itself would make front page news, and it would be very difficult to kill the bill once that happened. Byers left looking worried.

Three kinds of witnesses testified before the council. The Department and I brought in several pages of amendments, strengthening our own bill, which we had drafted during the six months of the "public pressure" campaign; some of these amendments had been suggested by groups such as the City Bar Association, others were our own design. Several unions and civic groups testified at our request, generally supporting the measure. The major business and trade associations realized that overt opposition would only harm their image, so they testified that they supported the bill "in principle," but that they objected to certain details of the proposal, and submitted to the committee chairman several pages of amendments designed to remove the bill's teeth. They did not submit any testimony or opposition to the new suggestions I had made, because they hadn't seen them before the hearing.

In his testimony, Byers stressed that he would be happy to sit down with the committee's staff counsel to work out language acceptable to the trade associations. I knew that such a meeting would be the bill's critical moment, and I also wanted the bill amended to include our new ideas, so at the end of the hearing I located the counsel, Ray Bushering, and requested that he call me at his convenience to get my views on the industry-sponsored amendments and to discuss my new proposals. He said he would call me, and Byers as well, when he was ready to work on the bill.

Several weeks passed, and I did not hear from Bushering. Meanwhile, the Commissioner kept up the pressure to report the bill out of committee; she telephoned the majority leader regularly, and although he didn't return her calls, he must have known what she wanted.

Meanwhile, Mayor Lindsay won a second term. With the election over, the bill's prospects were improved; the Democratic council would not be giving him political points by passing an administration bill.

After about four weeks, I called Bushering. He hadn't started to work on the bill yet, but he promised to call me within a day or two. He didn't call, so I called him again. He still was not ready.

After a while, the Commissioner began making a call every day. Then, suddenly, the logjam broke; Bushering told me that the committee would meet in executive session in three days to consider the bill. "Since you're the city's expert on this bill," he told me, "why don't you come along to the session?"

I told him that I would be happy to meet with the committee, but first I would like to see the amendments proposed by industry and find out which ones Bushering or the majority leader would recommend to the committee. I feared that the deal with industry had already been made.

Bushering told me that I could come down any time to see the file and discuss it with him. I was there in about half an hour.

He took out the file. I couldn't understand what was going on; it hadn't been touched since the hearing. There had been no meetings with industry. Gradually, I began to understand why; Bushering had told both Byers and myself that he would call us. But Byers had believed him, and had not been calling daily, as I had.

Bushering and I went through each of the proposed industry amendments, and I explained to him how each one was deftly designed to cripple the law. On a few minor points that didn't make much difference, I conceded; thus, I seemed fair and open-minded. Since Bushering didn't know much about the bill, and was impressed with my "expertise," he accepted virtually everything I told him.

When we finished with the industry proposals, I tried to explain the Department's new amendments to Bushering. He listened politely, but he was plainly tired and made no notes. That was a bad sign. He told me that he was not yet sure exactly when the executive session would be held.

Then, at about five o'clock a few days later, he called and said that the session would be held at ten the following morning. I told him I would come, but I would first like to know what he'd decided to do as a result of our meeting. He said he hadn't had a chance to work on the bill yet, but if I came down a few minutes before the executive session, we could make the final decisions with the committee Chairman.

I got to the council chamber at 9:00 A.M. The room began filling up, but neither the Chairman nor Bushering was there. I had dark visions of a secret meeting with Byers down the hall. Shortly after ten, another Councilman called the meeting to order, acting for the absent Chairman. Several other bills were also on the agenda, but I worried that the committee would reach and decide upon the consumer protection bill before I could even find out what was going on.

The Chairman and Bushering came in at about ten-thirty, and went immediately to the presiding officer's desk, so I had no chance to say even a word to them. I was mystified as to which of my amendments and which industry amendments the Chairman had decided to accept.

The other bills, fortunately, took a long time to work on. At 1:00, the session broke for an hour's lunch, with the consumer protection bill next on the agenda.

The instant the meeting recessed, I elbowed my way to Bushering. "What changes in the bill have you accepted?" I asked.

"Oh, we'll just pass the original bill," he said, his manner indicating that the decision was dictated by the fact that he never had gotten around to analyzing the amendments one by one, or going over the bill line by line.

"No amendments at all?" I asked.

"That's right."

"Look," I gasped. "There are a couple of amendments that we proposed that are really pretty important. Can I show you how I think the bill ought to look?"

"Sure," he said, "but first let's have some lunch."

He led me to a Deli-City across the street, a choice I warmly endorsed since it promised to cut eating time to a minimum. One eye on the wall clock, I swallowed my hot dog whole, thinking only of which amendments I should try to salvage at this last hour. Bushering, on the other hand, was in the mood for a solid meal. I nearly went looney watching him sip his coffee.

One thing I'd learned as a student editor is that power comes from the barrel of a staple gun, that almost anything can be rewritten instantly if you are handy enough with a scissors. So on our way back across the street, with twenty-five minutes to go, I asked Bushering for a clean copy of the bill, a scissors, and a stapler.

Back in his office, with twenty minutes to go, I began snipping and writing and stapling like mad. The Department's amendments went into the bill. The industry amendments remained neatly folded in a manila envelope. I also had a few new ideas as I went through the bill and stuck those in here and there. With two minutes to go, I showed Bushering a copy of the bill as the Department and I would like to see it passed.

"O.K.," he said, without reading it.

My delight at his easy manner was chilled more than a little by my astonishment and dismay at the process by which this bill was being written. This time, I figured, it was all right; I was the only one who knew everything that was in the bill, and I was a good guy. But this situation—the heroes writing the law and the villains frozen out—was a real fluke; usually, particularly in state legislatures, the lobbyists meet secretly with legislators and committee staff, and people like me aren't told what's going on until too late. I wasn't about to complain to Bushering, though.

I knew that this new bill was unlikely to pass unless I

could get copies to the eight or nine committee members; I asked Bushering if we could use the council's xerox machine. He said we could, so we went to the council reception area, where the machine was located. I put in the first page of the bill . . . and the machine failed to function.

Upstairs, the legislators were gathering in the chamber. The time was 2:03. I was kneeling on the floor, up to my armpits in the guts of the xerox machine, its secrets having been mastered during long nights at the Legal Defense Fund after similar mechanical failures.

The machine restored, the copies made, the clock running, I discovered that the Council of the City of New York had no collating machine, nor even a large table for collation.

2:09 P.M.: I was sitting on the red carpeted floor of the reception room of the New York City Council, distributing papers on nine little piles arranged around me in a semi-circle, stared at by secretaries, lawyers, guards, instructed to move out of the way; I was thinking about the film strips we used to see in junior high school on How Laws Are Passed, their cartooned legislators drafting, deliberating, meeting in committee, voting on precisely drawn amendments.

We got to the chamber as the meeting was coming to order, and distributed the copies. For an hour, I read the changes to the committee. Since I'd inserted dozens of amendments, it would have required many hours to debate them all, so the committee restricted its debate to two sentences, and, with my concurrence, changed the two sentences slightly. Then the Chairman moved committee approval of the bill, as amended, and it passed, without further discussion, with only one dissenting vote.

The majority leader then scheduled the bill for floor debate by the council on December 11, the following week; that session, I learned, was to be the final meeting of the council elected in 1965. Therefore, unless the bill passed at that meeting, it would have to be re-introduced in January, and we would have to start all over again. When I arrived at the December 11 meeting, both the industry lobbyists and I learned a startling fact; under a council rule, no bill can be amended on the floor during the last session of a council. The industry men were most unhappy to discover that the bill could only be voted up or voted down; it meant that they had no more chance to affect the legislation. The council passed the bill by a vote of thirty-four to nothing, and Mayor Lindsay signed it into law at a City Hall ceremony on December 30, 1969.[23]

NOTES

1. Comment, "Translating Sympathy for Deceived Consumers Into Effective Programs for Protection," 114 U. Pa. L. Rev. 395 (1966).

2. Technically, this term should only be used in the law of negotiable instruments, but courts have permitted a set of rights, analogous to the rights of the holder in due course, to be given to the third-party purchaser of a contract containing a clause whereby the person who signs the contract waives against a third party the rights he would have had against the seller of the goods or services. In the jargon of consumer lawyers and anti-consumer lawyers, these rights are also spoken of as the rights of a "holder in due course." In New York, such rights with respect to consumer contracts (other than for the sale of motor vehicles) have been governed by Personal Property Law Section 403, which permitted the harsh extinction of consumer rights by fine-print contract clauses until the law was amended in 1970 with respect to contracts signed after February 1, 1971.

3. American Bar Association, Report of the Commission to Study the Federal Trade Commission 20 (1969).

4. Ibid. at 24.

5. Cox, Fellmeth, and Schulz, The Nader Report on the Federal Trade Commission 59 (Black Cat ed. 1970).

6. Cox, Fellmeth, and Schulz, The Consumer and the Federal Trade Commission, Cong. Rec., 91st Cong., 1st Sess. 1539, 1547 (January 22, 1969).

7. See, e.g., Senator Joseph Tydings' description of the FTC's 29-year action against the Holland Furnace Company in Cong. Rec., 91st Cong., 1st Sess., S 4163 (daily ed., April 25, 1969).

8. Cox et al., supra n. 5, at 141.

9. Ibid. at 150.

10. Ibid. at 153.

11. ABA Commission Report, supra n. 1–4, at 33.

12. See Center for the Analysis of Public Issues, The New Jersey Office of Consumer Protection—A Promise Unfulfilled (1970); Kripke, "Gesture and Reality in Consumer Credit Reform," 44 N.Y.U. L. Rev. 1, 44–46 (1969).

13. In New York, most OEO neighborhood legal services offices reject consumer cases even if the complainant has no funds at all; for them, keeping up with welfare problems, divorces, and evictions is a full-time job.

14. See Caplovitz, Debtors in Default (Columbia University Bureau of Applied Social Research 1971), pp. 11–5 to 11–29; Comm. on Legal Assistance, Assn. of the Bar of the City of New York, "Does a Vendee Under an Installment Sales Contract Receive Adequate Notice of a Suit Instituted by a Vendor?" 28 Record of A.B.C.N.Y. 263 (1968); Public Hearings, Abuses in the Service of Process, Before Louis J. Lefkowitz, Attorney General, January 13, 1966.

15. Caplovitz, supra n. 15, at 11–30 to 11–67.

16. Schrag, "Bleak House 1968: A Report on Consumer Test Litigation," 44 N.Y.U. L. Rev. 115 (1969).

17. S. 1599 (90th Cong.).

18. American Home Improvement Co. v. MacIver, 201 A.2d 886 (N.H. 1964); Jones v. Star Credit Corp., 298 N.Y.S.2d 264 (S. Ct. Nassau Co. 1969), and cases cited therein.

19. City of New York, Local Law No. 68 of 1968.

20. The $50 minimum civil penalty was a deliberate attempt to avoid the "housing code trap," whereby judges frequently undercut housing code enforcement by fining offenders $5. We hoped the agency would cumulate violations and seek substantial fines which the courts could not nullify.

21. During the campaign, the Mayor appointed each Commissioner as Chairman of an "Urban Action Task Force" for a region of the city. The Task Forces held community meetings and provided contact between neighborhoods and City Hall. Commissioner Myerson's area was the largely Jewish section of Queens made up of Forest Hills, Kew Gardens, and Rego Park. In the 1969 election, the Mayor's opponents pictured him as the kingpin of a "Manhattan arrangement"; it was important for him to show strength in at least one other borough. He carried Manhattan overwhelmingly, and lost every other borough except Queens, where the vote in Miss Myerson's Task Force area accounted for his narrow victory in that borough.

22. The committees of the council also have some staff assistance.

23. City of New York, Local Law No. 83 of 1969.

2 · The
Civil Service

DURING THE TIME that I was writing and lobbying for the Consumer Protection Law, I did not expect to participate in its administration. But while the prospect that the bill would become law continued to increase, my test cases became further mired in irrelevant procedural molasses. The week after the bill passed, Commissioner Myerson asked me to join the Department to direct its enforcement, and by that time the decision seemed easy. I could continue to shepherd the cases through interminable motions, hoping to discover a judge who cared, or I could turn them over to a less weary lawyer and experiment with what could be an ideal alternative device for consumer law enforcement, certainly an ideal law. I agreed to join the Department on the condition that the city provide adequate funding for a law enforcement staff, by which I meant an annual budget of at least half a million dollars. The Commissioner went to bat for the money, but found the Mayor's office spectacularly reluctant to provide any appropriation whatsoever to enforce the law. The Mayor's office, particularly the Bureau of the Budget, was the pertinent target of her demands, because in New York the City Council has delegated to the Mayor not only the legislative process, but the appropriations process as well. Once each year, the council passes a city budget, appropriating sums by agency, but the amounts it allocates are of only minor importance because the Mayor directs each agency to spend only 80% to 90% of this money. The balance becomes the agency's "forced accruals" and "voluntary accruals" (two accounts are kept, but there isn't much difference between them), which must be returned to the treasury at the end of the year so that when some agency (e.g. the Bureau of the Budget) overspends, the city's budget remains balanced, and funds are always on hand for emergencies. Theoretically, an agency could go to the council and ask for a larger appropriation, but this would not help because the Mayor's office would direct that agency not to spend the additional money.

For a long time, City Hall refused to fund the program. In a city with an eight-billion dollar budget, half a million dollars is a very small amount of money—that much is probably lost every year in arithmetic errors. However, the city does have a chronic, massive budget problem, and must constantly battle over salary scales with unions representing the uniformed services. It cannot afford to grant even small raises in pay scales, because to do so for any significant fraction of the city's 400,000 workers would throw the budget off badly. Since it is very difficult to plead poverty during collective bargaining negotiations while granting funds to start new programs, there aren't any new programs, even small ones.

Finally, after an impassioned personal appeal from Commissioner Myerson to the Mayor, the Bureau of the Budget agreed to let the agency spend $100,000 on the new program, on the condition that it save an equal amount of money for the city by not filling vacancies as they occurred among weights and measures inspectors. Diminution in the authorized work force was a condition that the Bureau of the Budget frequently imposed when acceding to a Commissioner's request for permission to alter a program. In the Department of Consumer Affairs, this resulted, over an eighteen-month period, in a decrease in the weights and measures inspectorial force—through retirements, resignations, and transfers—from 200 men to fewer than 80 men.

However, the city does not really allocate *money* to agencies; it allots them specific *lines*. Departments have very little discretion about how to use their budgets; the Bureau of the Budget tells an agency that it may have, say, sixteen lawyers, four economists, sixty-five inspectors, two bookkeepers, three clerks, two stenographers, and a messenger boy. The $100,000 was enough to pay for me, two lawyers, two investigators, two secretaries, and the use of a stenotype service. Commissioner Myerson used a standard dodge to supplement this; she assigned to my Division a number of then vacant lines from other parts of the Department. For example, we put one investigator on a cashier's line; my Deputy, an experienced lawyer, had the civil service title of Senior Kosher Meat Inspector.

Unfortunately, wages are paid at the scale of the line, not that of the job being performed. Persons offered jobs on spare lines at salaries below those of their colleagues doing the same work in the same agency tended to object because they did not understand the system. Commissioner Myerson comforted them by explaining that at one time the Central Park Zoo had only one lion, which was getting so old and tired that it disappointed spectators by its sleepy manner. The zoo therefore bought a young lion, which it put in the cage with the older animal. At feeding time, the zookeeper gave the old lion a juicy steak, but threw the young lion only a banana and an orange. The young lion, disappointed, concluded that he hadn't performed well enough. So the next day, he paced behind the bars and growled and yelled. The spectators were delighted; they crowded around with great interest. But at meal time, once again the old lion got a steak while the new lion was given only an orange and a banana.

The new lion was very distressed; he decided that still he hadn't met the zoo's standards. The next day, he put all his energy into acting for the crowd. He showed his teeth, he growled, he roared, he chewed the bars. For dinner, when the old lion got his steak, the young lion got only a banana and an orange.

The young lion, on the verge of tears, called out to the zookeeper. "Are you so unhappy with me?" he asked. "Can't I make the grade?"

"Oh," said the zookeeper, "it's nothing to do with you. You see, we wanted a second lion, but we only had a line for a monkey."

Fortunately, we did not have to rely entirely on monkeys' lines; over the course of the next year, we were able to obtain federal grants to expand the Division and to open several neighborhood complaint offices. The city's seed money proved sufficient; by the time I left the Law Enforcement Division, it was operating with more than half a million dollars and had forty-two employees.

Contending with the Civil Service System was our major challenge. Very few jobs in the city of New York are exempt from competitive civil service examination. The lawyers of the Corporation Counsel (the city's Law Department), for example, are hired through civil service. I was quite sure that the lawyers who took such examinations, or even the ones who did well on them, were not the ones I wanted. I thought we should hire very young, aggressive, imaginative *kids,* both as lawyers and as investigators, that a history of participation in the civil rights or peace movements, or a stint in the Peace Corps or VISTA, for example, was a strong plus for a candidate. But the people who wrote civil service examinations were unlikely to agree with me.

I was particularly afraid that if the lawyers were to be civil service lawyers, they would be classified as "attorneys" under the civil service rules, and would have to be hired from the list of people who take the regular civil service test for "attorneys" of the city government—people who would just as soon be lawyers for the Tax Bureau, the Social Services Department, or the Police Department. While such persons might be highly qualified attorneys, they were unlikely to have the motivation I was seeking.

Our first step was to request that the Mayor's office exempt the entire new Law Enforcement Division from civil service classification and examinations. City Hall quickly replied that this request was ridiculous, and that at best, only my own job would be non-competitive.

Then we devised a two-pronged strategem: to distinguish our lawyers' jobs from those of city lawyers generally, we would describe the requirements for the position so technically that the Bureau of the Budget, the Department of Personnel, and the Civil Service Commission would perceive it as unique. Secondly, to prevent those agencies from giving tests for the new jobs we were creating, we would create not one job, but a great many, each with a different job description. The civil service agencies, already a year behind in their work, would never write a test for a position in which there was only one job, so we were far more likely to avoid testing if we offered thirty different kinds of jobs than if we had thirty openings for the same type of job. Each time we hired a lawyer, we would place him in an entirely new category.

It took the better part of a weekend to write formal job descriptions for thirty jobs, each different from the job of attorney, each different also from each other. The result was an unconscious parody of typical job specifications actually in effect for dozens of agencies throughout the city. A few examples from our submission to the Budget Bureau:

SENIOR CONSUMER FRAUD SPECIALIST—Assumes primary responsibility for administering those sections of the Consumer Protection Act relating to deceptive practices in areas other than unconscionability and consumer credit. . . . Authorizes and supervises investigation of complaints where litigation is not needed. . . . Supervises the Consumer Fraud Specialists, the Deceptive Discount Research Associate, the Trade Disparagement Examiner, the Bait and Switch Advertising Examiner, the Deceptive Food Labeling Investigator, the Advertising Language Analyst, and the other specialists with respect to that portion of their work involving deceptive prac-

tices. *Qualifications:* A baccalaureate degree, expertise in consumer deception and deceptive trade practices as demonstrated to the Commissioner of Consumer Affairs, and two
years legal training [if we'd said three, it would have looked
like we wanted an attorney].

SUBSECTION "D" INJUNCTION ADMINISTRATOR—Analyzes ongo-
ing violations in depth and recommends seeking of the appropriate type of injunctive order. . . . Supervises the Section
Five Assurance Negotiators and the Discontinuance Assurance Administrator with respect to injunctive aspects of Section Five assurances. . . . Where appropriate, orders field investigations or research into particular problems presented by
a particular complaint. *Qualifications:* A baccalaureate degree,
expertise in the field of injunctions as demonstrated to the
Commissioner of Consumer Affairs, and two years legal education.

UNCONSCIONABILITY SPECIALIST [A line for an investigator, not
a lawyer]—Detects and investigates current unconscionable
schemes and drafts regulations specifically dealing with the
unconscionable elements thereof. . . . Acts as liaison between
the Department and industry in a cooperative effort to eliminate unconscionable sales practices. . . . Conducts on-going
research into unconscionable sales practices in New York
City, including analysing firm and industry pricing structures
in relation to selling practices, market conditions, and firm
clientele. *Qualifications:* A baccalaureate degree, understanding of the concept of consumer unconscionability as demonstrated to the Commissioner of Consumer Affairs, familiarity
with court decisions construing Section 2–302 of the Uniform
Commercial Code, and any decisions construing Section
2203–2.0(b) of the Consumer Protection Act as demonstrated
to the Commissioner of Consumer Affairs, and negotiating
and drafting ability as demonstrated to the Commissioner of
Consumer Affairs.

One spring day, Commissioner Myerson and I went to
see Herbert Schwartz, the man in charge of job specifications, who had entered service for New York City as a clerk
and had risen, over thirty-four years, to the highest-ranking

non-political job in the city. He said, "You've got to be kidding."

"Is there something wrong with our job specifications?" asked the Commissioner.

"Buncha clowns," said Schwartz.

"We need very specialized talents," she added.

"Well, you'll never find them. These people don't exist."

"They do," I insisted. "These are the young lawyers you read about in the papers, dedicated to the public interest, who . . ."

"I know the type," interrupted Schwartz. "They come to the government, work a couple of years, then bingo, they're gone. No more dedication."

"Even if they do leave," I said, "that's all right. We'll get them at the peak of their enthusiasm. Then we'll replace them with other young people."

"Listen," said Schwartz, a kindly look in his eye, the look of a man who had been through all this many times before and was about to let me in on the Big Secret. "We can't have people like that working for the city. We want career people, who will stay twenty, twenty-five years, not these kids on their way through. Ya know why?"

"Actually, I don't," I admitted.

"Because in just one or two years they don't build up any equity in the pension fund."

Now I was mystified. "So what?"

"We don't want people with no equity in the pension fund," he said. "We want people who build up ten, fifteen years equity, a substantial amount of money due them from the pension fund."

"But what difference does that make?"

Schwartz answered slowly, beating his words out with one finger. "A man with ten years equity in the pension fund doesn't put his hand in the till, 'cause he can lose his pension rights."

"But these young lawyers aren't thieves!"

"Everyone near the till is a potential thief," said Schwartz. "That's why we have civil service. We lock 'em in; they have to stay with the city forever."

Evidently, I was making matters worse. The Commissioner interrupted and changed the subject. When we got back to the question of job specifications, I kept my mouth shut and let her handle it.

We came away from the meeting with half a loaf. The lawyers would not be classified as "attorneys," so they would not be chosen from the same list as all other lawyers who work for the city. But only three job titles would be created for the division—"Consumer Specialist" for the college-educated investigators, "Senior Consumer Specialist" for the lawyers, and for myself, probably the most exotic official civil service title in the city, "Consumer Advocate." Some day, tests would be written for these positions, but we would be consulted on what types of questions would be asked. Meanwhile, we would be free to hire anyone we pleased. In this case, the snail's pace of the city's bureaucracy worked to our advantage; a year and a half later, no one had even begun to design a test, and the Commissioner was still free to hire at will.

We put together a fantastic group of people. For lawyers, I went primarily to the Columbia Law School's class of 1970, which was about to graduate. The previous fall, I'd taught a seminar in consumer protection at the school, and I was able to persuade several of my best students to join us upon graduation. Each lawyer was assigned an investigator; the investigators were generally returned Peace Corps volunteers or refugees from corporations. Each month, as we got wealthier, we added staff—paraprofessionals, law students, various kinds of assistants. Our median age, however, remained about twenty-six.

Since we were starting a new type of agency, we did not want to begin by developing a rigid set of procedures; instead, almost everything we did was experimental, and the agency is still in the process of deciding what works and what doesn't, what is economical and what is not, what can be justified and what cannot. We took our cases primarily from the inspectors who serve as the Department's complaint bureau; they operate a twenty-four-hour a day, seven day a week telephone and mail complaint center. This bureau takes in over 20,000 complaints a year. The inspectors themselves resolve the routine problems by telephone mediation. But after the Law Enforcement Division was created, they referred the serious problems to us, particularly the companies generating huge numbers of complaints. We also got some cases from disgruntled employees who sought us out to spill the beans about the companies they worked for, and we sporadically monitored media advertising. At any given time, we had approximately 70 companies under investigation, and during a year we investigated a total of 180 companies, involving over 2,300 individual consumer complaints. We obtained sixty-five out-of-court settlements (formal assurances of discontinuance requiring companies to change their selling, advertising, or collection practices) and were involved in eleven court cases. Some of the settlements were major, some minor; together they enabled affected consumers to cancel contract obligations and to get refunds of over two million dollars, if they chose to exercise rights of which they were notified.

These statistics, however, do not tell the more important and vexing story of the Law Enforcement Division's disenchantment with a traditional model of law enforcement and its conversion to a more aggressive one. The balance of this book recounts six investigations typical of the work of the Law Enforcement Division, which illustrate the legal, practical, and moral problems we encountered, and the evolution of our strategic thinking.

When we began to operate, we had in mind a model of law enforcement procedure that might be called the "judicial" model. In this model, the law enforcement agency interviews witnesses, gathers the facts, presents the facts and the issues to a court, and asks the court to dispense justice. In such a system, the only contact between the agency and the defendant prior to litigation might be testimony by the prospective defendant's officers pursuant to investigative subpoena. Chapters three, four, and five are studies of three cases that may be classified under this "judicial" model.

In reaction to the frustrations we encountered in "judicial" model cases, we gradually evolved an altogether different "direct action" model, by which the agency, instead of or in addition to going to court, made a determination that a company was engaging in very bad practices and then sought out non-litigious ways to pressure the company into changing them. In other words, instead of participating as advocates in a two-party court contest, we and the company participated as two of many actors in the marketplace generally. For example, the judicial model could not include urging mass media to refuse advertising from a particular seller, at least not until a court judgment had been obtained against it. But such a tactic might be central in a "direct action" case. Chapters six, seven, and eight describe "direct action" cases undertaken by the Division.

Of course, these are polar models, and probably no case involved actions that could be classified exclusively as those of one model or the other. It is nevertheless possible to distinguish among the cases according to the strategy we employed; unfortunately, it seems as easy to distinguish among them according to the efficacy of our intervention.

3 · Delay:
The Case of the
Wigs and the Witness

WHEN THE DIVISION began to operate late in the spring of 1970, I asked the Department's inspectors to refer to us the companies which generated, relative to their size, the most complaints. Every inspector was quick to ask us to take over the case of Enchanting Wigs, Inc. a small mail-order house which at that time had already generated more than twenty-five complaints, within a few months, from consumers all over the country. Enchanting, it seemed, placed small advertisements in nationally circulated movie magazines and sensational weekly newspapers for wigs ranging in price from $4.99 to $30. It listed a Fifth Avenue address. The complaints, almost all of them handwritten, many in the shaky hand of an elderly correspondent, alleged that the customers had sent checks and money orders (of which copies were usually enclosed), often for two or more wigs, and that months later, their checks had been cashed but no wigs had been received. In some cases wigs were received, but not the sizes and styles that had been ordered. The customers' letters and long-distance calls to Enchanting yielded no response. It seemed like a simple case—Enchanting deceived people by taking their money and promising, falsely, to mail them certain merchandise.[1]

However, we had two steps to take before we could rush into court. First, we wanted to hear Enchanting's side of the story, in case it was not as simple as it seen.ed, and to hear what its defense might be. Second, very few of the complainants lived in New York. To prove that Enchanting did not in fact deliver the wigs, we would have had to fly witnesses to New York from all over the country, to make them available for cross-examination. We had no funds for such an operation. We therefore needed to prove Enchanting guilty from its own records and testimony.

We gave the case to Marjorie McDiarmid, a petite, serious young lawyer, the day she graduated from law school. Enchanting's certificate of incorporation listed its incorporator as Dr. Wesley Steele. Since his name did not appear in the telephone book, Miss McDiarmid started by going to the Fifth Avenue address to have a look at Enchanting. The office building was little more than a hulking shell on lower Fifth Avenue, far from the classy department stores that give the street its national reputation. When McDiarmid could not find an office in the building belonging to Enchanting, she identified herself as an employee of the Department of Consumer Affairs, and made inquiries of a man operating a telephone switchboard in the lobby. He showed her a shabby, unused room, containing only an empty desk, a chair, and an old desk calendar. The building, he explained, was used by dozens of companies as a mail drop; they each rented a one-room office, and sent someone once a day to pick up their mail and messages. His switchboard was an answering service for those tenants who wanted to use it. A woman with a Central European accent came in every day to get the Enchanting mail and to get her messages from him; the number for Enchanting in the Manhattan telephone book connected to his switchboard. He did not know the woman's name.

Unable even to find the company, much less learn its secrets, McDiarmid made plans to return one morning the next week, wait for the woman, and follow her. But that evening, re-reading the complaints, she found that one of Enchanting's customers had learned from a magazine in which Enchanting advertised that the ad had been placed by a company called the RBC Corporation. So on her way to work the following day, McDiarmid went to the offices of RBC, on the seventh floor of a midtown office building. She knocked on the door, and after a long wait, an emaciated blond woman opened it a crack and put her eye to the door. Behind the woman lurked a bulldog.

McDiarmid said that she was from the Department of Consumer Affairs and wanted to know about Enchanting Wigs.

"We don't know anything," snapped the woman. "We don't have any dealings with them."

"May I come in?" asked McDiarmid.

"You certainly may not," said the woman.

Peering above and around the woman as best she could, McDiarmid saw stacks of cardboard boxes in the room with the bulldog, not usually the props of an advertising agency.

"Well, may I have your name?" she asked.

"Merle Stanton," said the woman, slamming the door.

Stanton? Steele? A possible link to be stored for future use.

McDiarmid went straight to the Fifth Avenue Enchanting office. "The woman who gets the mail . . ." she said, a bit breathlessly to the switchboard operator. "Let me describe her to you."

"Sure," said the man.

"Tall and blond."

"Yep," said the man.

"About forty-five, skinny, bony even."

"That's her."

"Why are you so willing to help me?" asked McDiarmid.

"Enchanting's two months behind in paying for the answering service."

Back at the office, Miss McDiarmid sought out the inspectors who had been dealing with Enchanting and entreated them to search their memories for any further scraps of information about the company. One recalled that in trying to resolve a complaint against Enchanting, he had once managed to reach a company employee named Douglas Weller, who had given the inspector his telephone number and had promised to take care of the complaint. Weller never did resolve the complaint, so the inspector had done more digging and had found out that Weller also used another name, Rudy Berg. McDiarmid quickly found that the telephone number given by Weller was the one listed in the phone book for RBC.

She then checked RBC's certificate of incorporation filed with the New York County Clerk; its incorporator, too, was Dr. Wesley Steele. The certificate listed his home address, an apartment in the east seventies.

I authorized the issuance of subpoenas to Wesley Steele, Douglas Weller alias Rudy Berg, Merle Stanton, and "Mrs. Steele," and Miss McDiarmid set out to find them so that the subpoenas could be handed to them personally as required by law.[2]

McDiarmid went to the Steele apartment; one of the mail boxes in the lobby said "Steele—Berg." She located the superintendent and described Merle Stanton. The superintendent confirmed that a person of that description lived in the Steele apartment, 4–E. However, several attempts to serve a subpoena at that address during the day proved fruitless; no one was home. Finally, Miss McDiarmid taped the subpoenas for Dr. Steele and Douglas Weller to the door. She saved the subpoena intended for Mrs. Steele, the most crucial witness; it was most critical to serve that one personally, so there could be no dispute about its validity.

That evening, around eight o'clock, McDiarmid went with a male friend to the Steele apartment. The subpoenas were still taped to the door, but someone had obviously come

in since her visit earlier that day: sitting in the corridor, tied
to the Steele doorknob, was a familiar bulldog.

"Hi, bulldog," McDiarmid said. "Nice bulldog."

With one eye on the hound, she rang the bell. No one answered. McDiarmid and her friend sat down in the dark corridor, just beyond range of the dog, and laid siege to the
apartment, playing gin rummy, occasionally patting the dog
or ringing the doorbell.

After about half an hour, a male voice called from inside,
"Go away. Get out of here."

"Is Mrs. Steele or Mrs. Stanton home?" asked McDiarmid.

"Miss Steele ain't home. Get out of here," said the voice.

"Could we come in?"

"Did you hear me? Get out!"

"When do you expect Miss Steele?"

"She's not expected," said the voice. "She's in Europe."

McDiarmid and her friend continued to play gin rummy
and pat the dog. An hour passed, then two. Around eleven,
they decided to give up and call it a night. They put away
the cards, said goodbye to the dog . . . and heard footsteps
coming up the stairs. A tall, bony blond woman—Mrs. Stanton.

"Are you Miss Steele?" McDiarmid asked.

"Yes, I am," said the woman, startled.

"Well, here's a subpoena for you."

The woman took the paper and the two dollar witness fee
and disappeared without a word into the apartment.

The next day, to gauge the magnitude of the Enchanting
operation, McDiarmid called the various newspapers and
magazines in which it advertised, and asked how much
money it spent each month on advertising. "Oh, Enchanting," each one said, "they never pay their bills on time, they
owe us for months. But why do you want to know?"

"We're investigating some complaints from Enchanting's
customers," she said.

"You have gotten complaints? So have we," they volunteered. "As a matter of fact, we've just decided to refuse their advertising from now on."

Although the subpoena form had advised Miss Steele of her right to counsel, she appeared alone at the Department's offices on the date of the hearing. She hadn't understood, she said, that we'd wanted her to bring a lawyer. Her lawyer, she told us, was Dr. Steele, who was in Europe indefinitely. She also hadn't understood that she was required to bring the business records listed in the subpoena, so she'd come without them. The witness did admit that she was the person who actually managed Enchanting and that its operations were conducted from the offices of RBC, an advertising agency she also managed. She explained the complaints we'd received by saying, "I don't cheat anybody. But I employ mainly foreign girls, to give them a chance in America. They aren't always very bright, and they don't speak English very well, so they get orders mixed up and sometimes send wigs to the wrong address."

Most of the questions we asked dealt with her business methods and sources of supply; she refused to answer on the ground that she was not represented by counsel, or stated that she did not know the answer. We were trying to determine who her suppliers were, so that we could learn from them how many wigs they sent her. By comparing her physical supply with her records of orders, we might be able to determine that she accepted more orders than she intended to fill. However, this line of questioning, among others, was fruitless, because although she said she had "many" suppliers, she would not name them on the ground that her attorney was not present.

Finally, we agreed that she would return a week later with counsel, and that meanwhile we would deliver to her, at RBC, a letter specifying in detail the documents she was to bring with her, including, for each of our complainants, original order forms, books showing receipt of the money, proof of mailing the wigs, and any correspondence with the consumer.

Although Miss Steele had failed to bring the business records requested in the subpoena, she had brought copies of money orders, dated weeks before service of the subpoena, which, she said, represented refunds that had been mailed to our complainants.

During the week, McDiarmid checked with the bank on which the money orders had been drawn, and discovered that in every instance the money order had actually been purchased after the subpoena was served on Miss Steele; she had back-dated them so that it would seem to us that the refunds had been made voluntarily in the regular course of business.

By examining the canceled checks sent to us by consumers, we were also able to locate the bank in which Enchanting made its deposits. We asked that bank for copies of Enchanting's signature cards and monthly statements; they agreed, on the condition that we protect them from their client by serving them with a subpoena, a request with which we complied.

The signature cards indicated that the officers were: "President: [illegible squiggle], Vice-President: Rudy Berg a/k/a Douglas Weller, Secretary, Martha Steele, a/k/a Merle Stanton." The monthly statements were equally interesting: Enchanting made dozens of small deposits every week, and as soon as the account built up to fifteen hundred dollars or so, it would withdraw all the money. We prevailed upon the bank to give us microfilmed copies of the checks drawn by Enchanting. They all had the same payee: cash.

A week later, on the appointed date for the resumption of the hearing, Miss Steele did not appear. We called her office at RBC, but the telephone rang without answer. Enraged, we quickly drew up motion papers to enforce the subpoena in court. This step was necessary because in New York, violation of a subpoena issued by an agency is not contempt of

court. The agency must move for an order compelling compliance, and if that order is granted and then violated, the
respondent is in contempt.[3] The court may impose a fifty dollar fine, but it never does so. This procedure gives a subpoe-
naed party two bites at the apple, so many people ignore subpoenas.

At that time, the city's Law Department, the Corporation
Counsel, handled the Department's litigation—only later, in
an unusual political battle, did we obtain the right to go to
court ourselves. Early in July 1970, we gave the papers we'd
drawn up to the Corporation Counsel, which submitted them
to the court. Miss Steele's attorney filed a brief reply, claiming that she had a right to withhold the documents we demanded because they might contain "trade secrets." The
case was submitted in mid-July, and at our request, the Corporation Counsel asked that the case be expedited. By the
third week of August, we still had not read of any decision in
the official court newspaper, the *New York Law Journal.* So we
called the Corporation Counsel's office and asked them to
call the judge's chambers—perhaps the papers had been mis-
laid on a secretary's desk. The lawyer there refused; he said
he would call us when the decision came down.

Early in September, I called the Corporation Counsel
lawyer and renewed our request that he call the court. He
asked me, "Did you ever hear of that being done?"

I said I had; it was done all the time. The Corporation
Counsel had once done it for the Department in a case chal-
lenging one of our regulations.

"Did you win that case?" he asked.

"No," I said.

"See?" he declared. He refused to make the call.

A month later, no decision had yet been printed. This
time, the department's First Deputy Commissioner, Henry
Stern, called an executive in the Corporation Counsel's office
and requested that the call be made. The executive said that
that would be bad etiquette. Stern replied that he'd been a
clerk in the State Supreme Court, and that such calls were

made all the time, because papers are often accidentally buried in a pile on a secretary's desk. The executive confided
that the real reason they would not call was that the Corporation Counsel had a big case pending before this judge, and
they didn't want to use up capital by making too many requests of him.

Finally, a week later, the Corporation Counsel called the
court. The case had been decided August 7, more than two
months earlier, but through an oversight, had not been sent
to the *New York Law Journal* for printing.

In one respect, the decision was adverse to the Department; it held that we had to lay a firmer foundation for our
questions and our demands for records concerning Enchanting's sources of supply. But the court did order Miss Steele to
appear with the remaining records on ten days' notice, or at
a date set by agreement of the parties. Thinking that she
could obtain an agreement permitting her to interrogate
Miss Steele sooner than ten days, McDiarmid called Stanley
Gurinsky, Enchanting's lawyer. They agreed that Miss Steele
would appear on October 27, in the afternoon.

On the morning of the twenty-seventh, she called Gurinsky to confirm the hearing; Gurinsky told her that he was not
ready and would not appear that afternoon. She was an-
noyed, but reluctantly agreed to postpone the hearing until
the thirtieth.

On the afternoon of the thirtieth, neither Steele nor
Gurinsky appeared. McDiarmid called his office; he said
Miss Steele was sick. She informed him that the Department
had spent twenty dollars on a stenographic service that
would now have to be sent back; he said he was sorry. They
agreed to a postponed date of November 6.

She called him the morning of the sixth; this time he said
that Miss Steele refused to appear. She reminded him that
the court had ordered her appearance, and that violation
was contempt. He said he was sorry, but he couldn't force his
client to appear. I called Gurinsky and asked him to come
alone and explain his position; he came to the Department

and said that he would make every effort to obtain his client's compliance with the court's order. We set November 11 as a new date.

We sent him a letter confirming agreement on the eleventh as an adjourned date by agreement, and, to protect ourselves from any further procrastination, specifying formally the seventeenth as the tenth day after notice of hearing pursuant to the court order. We warned him that after that, we would apply for a contempt order.

We had become accustomed to the routine by now, so we didn't really expect Miss Steele to appear on the eleventh. She didn't. But we figured that we had insured her appearance on the seventeenth, and we kicked ourselves for trying to reach agreement at all rather than serving formal written notice at the outset.

On the morning of the seventeenth, McDiarmid called Gurinsky, this time certain that he would promise to produce his client that afternoon.

"I'm afraid I have bad news for you," he said, not sounding very unhappy about it. "I no longer represent Enchanting or Miss Steele. She has a new lawyer, a Mr. Ronald Speiser."

"They never told me about this in law school," McDiarmid mumbled to herself as she dialed Speiser. "Is Miss Steele coming here this afternoon?" she asked him.

"Of course not," he said. "I'm new on this case. I need time to prepare."

Ten minutes later, she sent him a new ten-day notice—actually a thirteen day notice—giving him until November 30 to produce Miss Steele.

On the thirtieth she appeared, but McDiarmid and Speiser did most of the talking during a three-hour hearing. They had long arguments on the record about the meaning of the court's order and the relevance of McDiarmid's questions and of the documents. By this time the number of complaints filed with the Department had risen to over thirty-five, but between Miss Steele's genuine or pretended failure to understand the questions, and her attorney's protestations, McDiarmid was able to cover only a single consumer's complaint. Miss Steele had not brought all of the documents covered by the order, and McDiarmid insisted that she do so the next week.

When Miss Steele appeared again a week later, only two consumer complaints were covered in another three hours of testimony. Again Miss Steele had not brought the documents which her attorney conceded were required by the court's order. He promised that she would deliver the documents to the Department the following week.

She failed to do so, so McDiarmid wrote a letter of inquiry.

There was no answer, so she wrote another letter, including a reminder that the hearing was scheduled to reconvene on December 29. On that date, neither Miss Steele nor Speiser appeared, and McDiarmid sent a new letter, to both of them, demanding their appearance, with the required documents, on January 12; she also demanded acknowledgment of receipt of the letter.

January 3 brought a telegram from Miss Steele: she would be delighted to appear on the twelfth.

And on January 12—a telephone call from Speiser: this time, *he* no longer represented Miss Steele.

"Why not?" asked McDiarmid, rising to a new level of anger.

"Because she hasn't paid my bill," said Speiser.

Miss Steele arrived without counsel, bringing still incomplete documentation for thirty complaints. (The total, meanwhile, had risen to forty-two.) She promised to bring the remainder on the fourteenth, but on that date she brought only incomplete documentation for the other twelve complaints, claiming she hadn't understood what we wanted. She promised to bring the rest of the papers on the twenty-sixth.

That hearing date was then adjourned to February 9,

which was confirmed in writing. But on the ninth, Steele again did not appear. McDiarmid called her, reached the answering service, but her call was not returned.

The next day, Miss Steele wandered in unexpectedly. She said she'd misunderstood the hearing date. She brought with her some, but not all, of the missing documents. Torn between her outrage and the time it was taking to compile the documents and her feeling that success was just around the corner, McDiarmid set a new adjourned hearing date, again demanded the balance of the papers, and waited. Once again the witness appeared, but without complete documentation.

This time McDiarmid gave up. She dismissed the witness and began the long, slow process of preparing the papers to commence a mass restitution action with the information on hand, attempting, as she did so, to construct a theory that would require presentation of a minimum number of consumer witnesses. Enchanting's customers, meanwhile, had been writing to us all spring, summer, fall, and winter, asking if we had forgotten them. By this time, their letters had dropped off. They had given up not only the prospect of obtaining satisfaction from Enchanting but of obtaining any assistance from what seemed to them a typical, uncaring government agency, so unresponsive or incompetent that it could not, in a year, solve the simplest sort of problem, such as obtaining a small refund for the disappointed purchaser of an undelivered wig.

As a lawyer representing individual consumers, such as Mr. and Mrs. Allen, I had often experienced delay in the legal process. But at the same time, I had been a bit awed by the power of government; I'd always assumed that lawyers opposing the government were also impressed, and that therefore, an attorney representing a city or a state experienced a better lubricated system of justice. I also assumed, when the City Council passed the Consumer Protection Law, that the powerful remedies which it gave to the city would further suggest to lawyers that the usual obstructive tactics were inappropriate. The Enchanting Wig case and others like it[4] dashed my hopes, and helped to "radicalize" the young lawyers who joined the Department. The truth of the matter is something like the old adage, "Possession is nine-tenths of the law." Whatever is happening tends to keep happening, and the person trying to use the legal system to make a change, whether he be private plaintiff or the government, faces an uphill struggle that is long and difficult, but often more long than difficult, though time may make the difference between success and failure.

As the months passed, we found that companies could almost always prevent us from doing our job if they were willing to fight hard enough, and that their most successful technique was their appearance of incompetence and their retention of obstructive counsel. We saw many different styles of obstruction; two of the most effective were the failure to return telephone calls and the frequent substitution of new counsel who needed time to prepare the case.

The theoretical remedies for defeating obstruction are unavailable in practice. For example, when Miss Steele continually refused to supply the required documents, we could at any time have applied to the court for a contempt order. But contempt orders are rarely given—in fact, they are virtually never given on the first application; the court holds that the respondent may be held in contempt, upon a new application, if he does not do such and such by a particular date. Meanwhile, weeks, often months, are lost in seeking the court ruling; the application to the court quite naturally freezes whatever cooperation might have been developing among opposing counsel. For us, going to court again would have meant a sure delay and a chance of losing; each of the many short adjournments seemed only a minor price to pay for possible compliance with the original court order. Our problem was that the short delays amounted, in the aggregate, to frustration of our investigation.

Perhaps the practical delays built into the process of investigating and remedying an alleged wrongdoing are actually an important safeguard of American liberty, akin to the presumption of innocence, which also at times permits the guilty to go free while it helps to protect the public from unwarranted conviction. Certainly the availability of obstructive or dilatory techniques tends to prevent the government, or, for that matter, anyone else, from making a successful blitzkrieg attack on an individual or company that is prepared to fight back. But there, I suppose, is the rub; while there is something to be said for slowing down the state's attempt to deprive a person of liberty or livelihood, not much can be urged for a device that is only available to those with the financial resources to put up a fight. Companies desiring to continue unlawful practices spend years in court; accused individuals who cannot afford more obstructive representation than is provided by overburdened, mass-production legal aid societies spend years in jail.

NOTES

1. The reader may well wonder why cases like this—and there are many of them—are not referred for prosecution as theft. The answer is that the District Attorneys refuse to prosecute because they do not believe that they can get convictions under N.Y. Penal Law § 155.05(d): "In any prosecution for larceny based upon a false promise, the defendant's intention or belief that the promise would not be performed may not be established by or inferred from the fact alone that such promise was not performed. Such a finding may be based only upon evidence establishing that the facts and circumstances of the case are wholly consistent with guilty intent or belief, and excluding to a moral certainty every hypothesis except that of the defendant's intention or belief that the promise would not be performed." We also checked with the United States Post Office early in our investigation of Enchanting: postal inspectors had been investigating Enchanting for five years but did not think that they could prove the company guilty of using the mails to defraud.

When convictions of white collar criminals *are* obtained, sentences are extremely light. The *New York Times* for October 31, 1971 reported the conviction of a collection lawyer who for five years had collected the same legal fees from his corporate clients and the consumers he sued in their be-half. He was fined $9,500 and given a six-month suspended sentence.

2. The law is maddeningly ambiguous about the validity of an easier means of serving a subpoena. It permits service of a *summons* by a combination of mail and affixation to the respondent's door where personal service cannot be made, and provides that a *subpoena* shall be served in the same manner as a summons. It also requires that proof of "nail and mail" service be filed within twenty days with the clerk of the court named in the *summons*. But no court is named in an investigative subpoena, and the clerks have no authority to accept for filing a proof of service of something other than a document pertaining to a suit. Furthermore, non-personal service is not valid until ten days *after* filing with the clerk. Therefore, we had some doubt as to whether "nail and mail" service of a subpoena was legal, and the City's Corporation Counsel advised us informally that only personal service would be valid. Compare N.Y.C.P.L.R. Sections 308(4) and 2303.

3. N.Y.C.P.L.R. Section 2308(b).

4. The Enchanting case does not hold the record for delay in the enforcement of one of our subpoenas. Later in the year, the District Attorney's office asked us to investigate the Oceanic Fur Company, which appeared to take furs for storage or reconditioning from low-income women, and then tell the women that the furs were in such bad shape that they'd fallen apart in the shop. To "compensate" the women, Oceanic sold them replacement furs, on credit, at a "discount." Meanwhile, Oceanic sold the original furs to someone else or pledged them as security for loans to the company. We issued a subpoena for various inventory records early in December 1970, returnable December 16. They moved to quash the subpoena, filing a short affidavit and no brief. We decided to brief the issue, and wanted the case to be heard early in January; their lawyer said he was going on vacation at that time, so we agreed to a court hearing early in February. Towards the end of January, we gave a draft of the brief to the Corporation Counsel; they wanted time to review it, so they had to agree on a new date with Oceanic's lawyer. Although we felt that any further adjournment should not exceed two weeks, Oceanic's lawyer insisted on an adjournment until the end of March, or none at all. Against our wishes, the Corporation Counsel consented to the eight-week adjournment. When the eight weeks had run, the Corporation Counsel decided they needed three weeks more to study our draft brief (which ran about ten pages). The case was finally submitted on April 20, and the court decided it, in our favor, nine days later. We then notified Oceanic formally of a hearing date, pursuant to the order in mid-May. On that day, no one appeared; we lost $20 for the transcription service, and we were furious. We called their attorney; he wasn't in, and his secretary said he must have forgotten about the hearing. The next day, he informed us that he was appealing the court order. We waited for a few days; nothing happened. So we applied for a contempt order. On the hearing date of that application, Oceanic's lawyer sent the judge a note saying that he was required to be in another court that day. The judge gave him another week, and eventually ruled that Oceanic had to appear late in June. At that time, we had to adjourn the

hearing for two weeks because our lawyer on the case was in Europe. When it was finally held, in July, their lawyer arrived an hour late, then made an opening statement which consumed the remainder of the afternoon. When our attorney was finally set to examine the witness, time had run out, and Oceanic's attorney insisted that his calendar was so full that he could not return until August. Since a court challenge or new contempt application would have taken even longer, our attorney agreed to the further postponement.

4 · Bureaucracy: The Case of the Lifetime Discount

THE TELEPHONE RANG. The resident, Dorothy Davis, answered.

"Hello. I'm Frank Bannerman, calling from the Wondra Corporation. I'd like to stop by and give you a free gift."

"Free? Don't kid me."

"Absolutely free! No obligation at all."

"Well. . . ."

"I'll be by at eight o'clock tomorrow."

He arrived on time. "Good evening, Bannerman is my name.[1] Bill and Mary Jones asked me to stop by. . . . I'd like to step in a minute if I'm welcome. . . . One of the things I want to talk about this evening is saving money. This is something we all talk about but few of us ever do anything about. And I think you'll agree that saving money is just as important as making money. Now, the way I'm talking about saving money is through a shopper's service and there's one thing I'd like to make clear at this point. THIS SERVICE IS NOT FOR SALE. YOU COULDN'T BUY IT AT ANY PRICE.[2] There are two primary reasons why a shopper's service saves its members both time and money. First of all, mass buying power. Thousands of families buying as a single unit to get the lowest possible quantity price. . . . The second reason is full-time professional shoppers. . . . A shopper's service gives advantages to its members much the same as Hertz or Holiday Inn receive.

"If, in the next year, you were able to buy almost every product you use, anything from aspirin to automobiles, through a shopper's service I'm sure you folks realize that you would have to save a great deal of money. The U.S. Department of Commerce tells us that the average American family spends over $5,000 each year maintaining a home and supporting a family. If you save just 10% you would have to save $500 a year. Now I know that I haven't given you any details, but on the strength of what I've told you, if you had a service like this would you use it?

"Now as I told you before, Mrs. Davis, this service is not for sale, but my company does allow me to give it to people under two conditions. First, that they would use it if they had it, and this you've already answered. The second is that you would recommend our product, and this you can't answer because you haven't seen it. . . . Is that fair enough? Fine, I'll step out to the car and I'll be right back."

Bannerman stepped out and returned with a large box. "I work for a local company who is the franchised distributor for Industrial Scientific Corporation, who has factories throughout the world. . . . You have heard of Lockheed, North American, Northrup, Douglas, and Boeing. During the war years, Industrial made precision parts and assemblies that contributed to the performance of aircraft manufactured by these companies. Industrial built the actuating cylinders that open and close the bomb bay doors on the B–29. They also built the entire fusilage for the Navy's AD–6 [and] the Hiller helicopter. After the war Industrial used its tremendous technical knowledge in supplying vital components for this nation's missile defense system on the Atlas, Nike, Jupiter. . . . I think you will agree that Industrial has a back-

ground as air specialists. I've been called an air specialist too
—a hot air specialist.

"What do you think I have in the box?"

Dorothy Davis could only imagine a helicopter or guided
missile.

"Now let me show you this complete, self-contained mul-
tipurpose home cleaning system."

Bannerman proceeded to open the box and demonstrate
the vacuum cleaner it contained. Most of the discussion that
followed, however, concerned not the machine but the "shopper's service"; Bannerman explained that by using it, a person could get anything he wanted, for the rest of his life,
wholesale. All Mrs. Davis had to do was walk into any store,
spot a product, tell Wondra about it, and Wondra would get
it for her, "with no middleman." Of course she had to sign a
contract for the vacuum cleaner, but she would quickly re-
coup its cost through savings realized with the shoppers' service. The one hitch: Mrs. Davis would have to make up her
mind right away; company policy did not permit offering the
shopper's service unless the customer signed up during Bannerman's initial visit.

"But I'd like to think it over."

"I'll tell you what I'll do, just for you, but don't tell my
company or I'll get in trouble. Just sign now, and I'll give
you my home phone number. I won't turn in the contract
until morning, so if you call me at home at nine o'clock tomorrow, I'll just tear it up."

Mrs. Davis signed, agreeing to pay $525 for the vacuum
cleaner and use of the shoppers' service.

At nine the next morning, she called Bannerman at
home, to cancel.

"Wondra Corporation," said a voice.

"Mr. Bannerman?"

"Not in."

"Is this his house?"

"This is *Wondra*, lady."

"He told me it was his house. I signed a contract last

night for a vacuum cleaner. It's much too much money. I want to cancel."

"You signed a contract?" said the voice. "Then you can't cancel. Contracts are binding and you'll be sued and your wages garnisheed if you don't pay."

"But Mr. Bannerman said . . ."

"Salesmen aren't authorized to permit cancellations," said the voice. "Anyway, by now your contract has been assigned to World Discount Corporation, a finance company. So it's got nothing to do with us any more."

Mrs. Davis was near tears.

She and her husband paid the first installment, figuring that there was nothing they could do. Perhaps, they figured, they *could* make back some of the money by using the shoppers' service. A few weeks later, they needed a new television, so they went to the local appliance store to select one.

The form that Wondra had sent them required them to list all the numbers on the back or bottom of an appliance they wanted to buy. When Mr. Davis tried inspecting the television he wanted, kneeling down so he could see what numbers were on the bottom, the manager threw them out of the store.

As the months rolled by, the Davises made more payments, and as the payments became more burdensome, they realized that they didn't dare use the shoppers' service and become further indebted to the company. Then Mr. Davis became sick and had to pay a large doctor bill; they could not afford to continue their monthly payments to Wondra. They stopped paying, and received a letter from World Discount Corporation threatening a lawsuit. The letter said that if World won a suit against Mr. Davis, it could garnishee his wages; Mr. Davis knew that his boss did not promote employees who got into trouble with creditors. In desperation, Mr. Davis, and several others like him, called the Department of Consumer Affairs.

Stephen Newman, another of our greenhorn lawyers,

began the investigation by collecting the stories of all the complaining consumers and having them sign affidavits telling what happened to them. Although each individual might have imperfect recollection on some of the points, the affidavits, taken together, gave a fairly clear picture of the sales technique.

To be absolutely sure that our complainants were telling us exactly what Bannerman and the other Wondra salesmen said, Newman also arranged for two of our paraprofessional investigators to be visited by Wondra salesmen. He hid tape recorders under their sofas and recorded the entire sales pitch. When he transcribed the tapes, he saw that the salesmen stated at least a dozen times that the discounts available to buyers through the shopping service were "lifetime, wholesale" discounts. One salesman told our investigator that the company was able to offer such good bargains by having several subsidiaries which sold in exactly the same way; that way, he said, it avoided the high income tax rate which applies to large corporations.

Newman also did some research into Wondra, and discovered that its President, Morton Glasser, had been in this business for many years, using various corporate names. Six years ago, while operating through the Wondramatic Corporation, he'd been sued by the New York State Attorney General for consumer fraud. A strong order had been entered against the company by the trial court, but an intermediate appellate court had modified the judgment by eliminating half the relief obtained by the Attorney General. Still, some injunctive relief had been obtained, and the Court of Appeals affirmed the intermediate decision. Then Glasser had switched corporations and also altered the nature of the scheme, so that he wasn't doing precisely the things forbidden by the court.

We issued a subpoena to Glasser, and he reacted with indignation. "Why subpoena me?" he asked. "I run an honest business. Just tell me who has complained to you about me and I'll let each one out of his contract, provided he gives back the vacuum cleaner, lets me keep his money, and pays me another twenty-five dollars as a penalty."

We were less than pleased with his offer for two reasons. First, a person who has been deceived should get all his money back, and our mission was to see to it that he did; Glasser was not offering refunds, and in fact was insisting on a penalty payment. But some of the consumers were desperately anxious to be relieved of their obligations to Wondra and would accept his terms.

That, at least, was their choice, and were that all to consider, we could leave it to them. But we knew that hundreds of persons were in the same situation as our few complainants, and hundreds more would be, unless we got Glasser to change his business practices. To do so, we thought, we had to sue him and present testimony from angry witnesses who had been injured by his salesmen. What would a judge think of our witnesses if months before the trial, Glasser had made settlements with each of them, which they voluntarily accepted?

With some moral anxiety, then, we advised the complainants not to settle with Wondra, and most of them agreed. We did not at that time tell Glasser who they were. Instead, we went ahead with the hearing.

It was almost comical: Stephen Newman, the most quiet, reserved, pleasant lawyer you could meet, asking simple questions of a sentence or two; Morton Glasser, high-pressure, super-salesman, gesticulating wildly, screaming out the answers, getting excited and having to be calmed down by his attorney, taking five or ten minutes to respond to each question, eager to sell Newman on the idea that his was a reputable company. He seemed to believe that at the end of the hearing Newman would buy a vacuum cleaner in order to get discount bargains.

His testimony revealed serious discrepancies between the salesmen's spiels, as evidenced by our affidavits and tape recordings, and the actual Wondra offer as authoritatively explained by Glasser. The discounts were not "wholesale" discounts; salesmen were specifically instructed not to refer to them as such. They did not apply to all products; food, house brands, and fair-traded items, for example, were excluded. Membership was not a lifetime proposition; it lasted one year, after which the consumer had to pay an annual fee to renew it.

Glasser also revealed that he personally owned all the stock in both Wondra and World Discount, and that World Discount was not a finance company and did not buy contracts from Wondra. Collection lawsuits were brought by Wondra itself; World was in the picture only to scare customers into thinking that they had been switched to an impersonal institution they could not cope with. World used, as its address, a post office box in another town, although its offices were really in the same building as those of Wondra.

We decided to sue Glasser and Wondra at once, but not for mass restitution. We felt that we might lose such a case, because the precise pitch used by each salesman might be sufficiently different from the others that the court would hold restitution inappropriate without an inquest into each individual case. We wanted to be certain to win an injunction, so we settled for requesting only that the deceptive practices be stopped.

At that time, the city's Law Department, the Corporation Counsel was still filing our court papers, so we had to submit them to that office. Newman and I drew up a summons, complaint, application for preliminary injunction, and six supporting affidavits—two from our paraprofessional investigators who had been visited.

On August 20, 1970, I took the papers, which I thought were complete, to Matthew Baker, Chief of the Enforcement Division of the Corporation Counsel. He noted that there was some urgency to this case, because we wanted to ask the court, on the basis of our affidavits and any counter affidavits Wondra filed, to enjoin Wondra's deceptive practices pending an eventual trial. He therefore promised action within a few days. When three weeks passed without word from

Baker, I called him. He assured me that he would have the papers ready for Commissioner Myerson to sign on Monday, September 21.

On Friday, September 18, Newman received a call from Preston Tanner, an attorney in Baker's division who had just been given the papers and assigned to prepare the case. Newman supplied the additional details Tanner requested, and told him that we were looking forward to having the suit commenced on the twenty-first.

Tanner said he had other important matters on his desk and couldn't do it by the twenty-first. He asked if the case was important. Newman reminded him that we were requesting a preliminary injunction because consumers were being cheated every day. Though he was surprised to hear that his office had been holding our papers for nearly a month, Tanner refused to promise action by any particular date.

A week later, Tanner asked Newman to visit him to discuss the case. Newman noticed that Tanner had inserted several yellow work sheets into the Commissioner's affidavit and asked to examine the changes. Tanner refused to show them to him, saying that the Corporation Counsel, not the Department of Consumer Affairs, was the city's lawyer, and the Department, as a client, did not have the right to review its attorney's work. At Newman's insistence Tanner agreed to show him one page, and though Newman pointed out an important omission, which Tanner restored, he was denied access to other changes. Tanner's final words were, "Don't call me; I'll call you."

On September 28, Tanner told Newman the papers would be ready the following day, but when Newman went to see Tanner, he claimed that the Commissioner's affidavit was being typed. Tanner also suggested that there would be further delay, pointing to a new case on his desk which he said had to be handled at once.

After another week with no action, I called Baker to remind him that six weeks had passed on a case in which injury was occurring every day. Baker said that the "final touches" of the typing were being done, and that it would be sent to Commissioner Myerson on that day or the next.

Newman pressed Tanner at noon on the following day. Tanner put him off once again, saying that he had several "rush cases." I called Baker to inquire further, but no one knew where he was. When I finally reached him the next day, he assured me that the complaint was being proof-read and would be given to us the next day, October 9.

At 5:00 P.M. on the ninth, a messenger brought carbon copies of the papers, but not the originals we had to sign. The twelfth was a holiday, so we telephoned our approval of the papers on the morning of the thirteenth. Although Baker's lieutenant promised delivery of the originals, that day or, at the latest, the next, they did not arrive. So on the fifteenth, I wearily called Baker, who promised that the papers would be sent that very day; he said they had been so badly typed that retyping was necessary, but there were many other cases in the steno pool. I called him again at 6:30, because they still had not arrived. He said he would look into it.

Tanner came to see me at noon the next day, with the papers. This was the first time I'd met him. He was a tall, distinguished looking gentleman, about fifty, with a carefully trimmed moustache. Right off the bat, he told me that he didn't approve of the Consumer Protection Law. "You're trying to solve all the problems of the world," he said. "That statute aims to be all-encompassing, it purports to end sin. You can't end sin with legislation."

"It's surely better to have such a statute than not to have it," I ventured.

"No," he said. "Statutes like that are harmful because they cause a lot of problems of interpretation. When you get to be my age you'll understand."

"But look at this case," I said. "Look at what these companies do."

"This is a borderline case," he replied. "These affidavits describe activities that may be legitimate business techniques. For example, your original draft of the complaint said that the salesman often stayed in the house for two-and-a-half hours. There's nothing wrong with that, so I had to take it out of the complaint."

Commissioner Myerson signed the affidavit, which was still poorly typed. Tanner said the affidavit (other than the last page, which she'd signed) would have to be retyped again, so I returned the document to his office for notarization and retyping. Later that day, Tanner called me to say that we would have to send someone to his office the following week to pick up the papers once again, because the Commissioner's signature hadn't been notarized.

"So just have a notary public in your office sign and stamp it," I said. "It's O.K. I saw her sign it. And anyway, you're retyping the entire document and stapling it to her signature."

"No," he said. "One of your notaries has to do it. Otherwise it would smack of illegality."

We picked up, notarized, and re-delivered the papers, and, a few days later, I called Baker to ask whether the papers had been served on Glasser. He told me they had been given to a process server, and he was waiting to hear that they'd been served.

Newman called Tanner a week after that to ask whether service had been made. Tanner, unaware of my earlier conversation with Baker, said that the exhibits to the affidavit still had to be mounted and the papers xeroxed, all of which would take a day or so. He said he had another urgent matter on his desk, but would get to the Wondra case "at the earliest opportunity."

Two more days passed. I called Baker to ask whether the papers had been served. He said that the process servers were having trouble finding Glasser. I recalled that our paraprofessional had had no difficulty serving him with a subpoena.

After another five days, Newman called Tanner to ask again. This time Tanner said that the papers would be given to the process server in a day or two. Finally, on November 4, seventy-six days after we'd submitted virtually final drafts to the Corporation Counsel, Glasser was served with the papers. The very next day, his lawyer called Baker and said Wondra wanted to consent to everything we demanded in our complaint.

Tanner told me that he would arrange a meeting to discuss settlement with Glasser and his lawyer, Edward McCrary. He said, "Schrag, I think this whole matter is an exercise in futility. You people are doing this to make yourself think you're doing something." I called Baker and said that in the settlement discussions we wanted to demand not only that Wondra stop its practices but that it make refunds, as well, to deceived consumers. Baker told me that to ask for refunds in the negotiations, when we had not made that request in our court papers, would be "legally improper." I said I thought that in a settlement, the parties could agree to anything they wanted to. He said that he was the lawyer and would have none of it.

The next week, Baker scheduled a meeting in his office. Tanner hadn't prepared a written set of demands, and Newman had, so we used Newman's, which was very strong. For example, we asked

> that Wondra disclose in its first contact with a customer that it was selling vacuum cleaners for $425 plus finance charges.
>
> that at the outset of the visit, the salesman make a binding oral estimate of how long, at most, he would stay in the prospect's house.
>
> that the salesman be required to leave if the customer said, "I can't afford it."
>
> that all misrepresentations cease.
>
> that Wondra send a questionnaire to all of its past customers, inquiring what the salesman told them, and refund money to those who were cheated.
>
> that Wondra send a questionnaire to all future customers, and instantly cancel contracts wherever a salesman has told a lie.

that Wondra fire salesmen who generate more than one complaint per year to the Department.

The meeting began: Baker, Tanner, Newman, myself, and Marjorie Smith, another of our new lawyers, on our side; Glasser and McCrary on theirs. They heard our demands; then Glasser and McCrary caucused privately. They returned and agreed to a decree prohibiting fraud, but nothing else. Glasser began warming up, yelling about the virtue and honesty of his company, trying to sell Baker a vacuum cleaner as he'd earlier tried to sell Newman.

Baker wanted to reach an agreement. He suggested going through the Department's demands one by one, and suddenly, he cast himself in the role of an arbitrator between the Department and Wondra; we wondered where our attorney had gone. He went through our list of demands very quickly, conceding them away one by one. Newman and I felt constrained not to fight with him in front of our adversaries.

One of the main sticking points was our demand that the salesman announce the purpose of his visit at the outset; Baker seemed willing to insist on this, but Glasser was adamantly opposed. "Look," he told Baker, indicating Marjorie Smith, "selling is like romancing a girl. You have to warm up the customer. When a young man takes a girl out for the first time, he says, 'Say, I'd really like to get to know you better.' He doesn't say, 'Baby, I'd like to squeeze your tits.' "

That must have persuaded Baker, who conceded the point.

All during this meeting, Glasser was pacing furiously, yelling. McCrary kept telling him to "relax, Mort. Sit down. Shut up."

At Baker's instruction, Tanner prepared a draft of a decree based upon the agreements reached at the meeting. Newman was stunned when he read it the next week; it was as if Tanner hadn't been at the meeting. Half of the points agreed to were missing; half of the points conceded away by

Baker were in the draft. Evidently, Tanner hadn't been able to take accurate notes in the helter-skelter settlement meeting. Seizing the situation, Newman restored the points that had been agreed to but were missing, and made no mention of the points that were erroneously contained in the draft. The result was his original list of demands.

Late in December, Tanner told Newman that McCrary had proposed that violations of the decree not be punishable as contempt, but, instead, that complaints would be subject to arbitration. Though Tanner recommended that we agree to this proposal, we refused, pointing out that it was a license to steal, provided the company settled with those few victims who complained.

The negotiations broke down over this point, and Wondra answered the motion of a preliminary injunction. In answering affidavits, Glasser denied that the company did any of the things alleged in our papers, but promised in any event, never to do them in the future. Wondra also tried to sell the judge a vacuum cleaner, though its claims were preposterous: "The buying service makes available a privately owned brand of concentrated bio-degradable household detergents. By purchasing these detergents, the member can save over 50% of their monthly household detergent bill, which can save approximately $100 each year on this commodity alone." The two salesmen who had given the pitch to our investigators swore that they had never made the statements charged. Of course, McCrary didn't know we'd made recordings.

We wanted to submit various reply papers to the court, such as (1) a demand for additional relief, including a demand that Wondra be ordered to give questionnaires to future customers to police compliance with the decree, (2) reply affidavits from the investigators, revealing the existence of the tapes and quoting them exactly, and (3) a brief. I called Tanner to explain.

Tanner refused to ask for the questionnaires. Such relief

would "restrain the man from his business practices," he explained. "Before you can do that you have to have a trial." I said the preliminary injunction would not be enforceable without this policing device, because Wondra sold to relatively low-income consumers, who rarely complained to the Department. When Tanner then said he couldn't get the necessary papers typed and copied in time, I said that we would do it. No, he said, only the Corporation Counsel could type and copy legal papers.

After I blew up at him, he said he'd tell me the *real* reason he would not ask for the relief: "We don't think it's wise." An appeal to Baker failed; the office seemed very reluctant to risk losing a case.

We also wanted to file a reply affidavit by one of our consumer complainants; Wondra had produced a statement signed by this customer saying that she was happy with the vacuum cleaner. In her reply, the complainant wanted to say that she'd signed it because the salesman had said that her doing so would gain him a promotion; he'd said that his young wife was ill and that he had five children, so she'd signed it at the time she signed the contract. Tanner refused to file that affidavit because, he said, he didn't believe it. We succeeded in getting Baker to put it in.

Meanwhile, one of the paraprofessional investigators who'd been visited had been dismissed by the Department. She was angry at us, so she refused to execute a reply affidavit. Newman went to see her at her new job in a Bronx hospital, and by pleading and begging, he persuaded her to give us the affidavit.

There was some further delay in submitting the case as the parties jockeyed for a judge they deemed acceptable. Each week a different judge hears motions, so by choosing a particular hearing date, the side making a motion can pick a judge. Then the other side can bump the case to another judge by demanding an adjournment on grounds of unpreparedness, illness, etc. This goes on until both sides agree, always tacitly, on a judge. In our cases, the purpose of this maneuvering was to avoid judges reputed to be "political" or "reachable," meaning that they could be bribed or influenced by political cronies. In four years of practice in the New York courts, I've never seen any evidence of bribery, but the practicing bar talks all the time in terms of judges being "reached," and this is a real and frequent factor in the timing of motions.[3]

At last all the legal papers were submitted to the court. Weeks passed, but we waited patiently, confident that the decision would stop the company from engaging in any further fraud. Late in March, the court issued its decision.

We could not have been more astonished by the court's ruling, which denied every part of our request. The judge commented that since Wondra had, in its court papers, agreed to refrain from committing any deceptive practices in the future, it would not be necessary to order their termination. And our demand that the company's salesman identify their purpose at the outset of their visit was denied because we could not demonstrate that the postponement of this disclosure, as opposed to other abuses, caused consumers to be entrapped into making purchases.[4]

The decision was a crippling blow. The court left it open to us to reapply for a new injunction if we found that Wondra was continuing to employ deceptive selling techniques. But that meant we had to begin our investigation from scratch; evidence of fraud collected before the decision was immaterial.

Since a year passed, on the average, between the time a fraudulent sale was made and the time that economic and legal pressure from Wondra's collection lawyer made it worth the consumer's while to complain, we would not be able to collect evidence of fraud from new complainants for some months. We did try getting more appointments for paraprofessionals to be visited, but Wondra was now on the lookout for ringers, and even though a few appointments were scheduled, the salesmen never appeared. Of course, the court contemplated that we would ask for a permanent injunction after a trial, but the court calendars are so crowded that no trial would have been possible for at least nine months, and pre-trial maneuvering often postpones trials for years.[5]

The effect of the court's decision was to give Wondra three bites at the apple instead of the usual two. Because the judge chose to rely on Wondra's promises of good behavior, new deceptive practices would not constitute contempt of court, but would merely lay the basis for yet another application for an injunction; to punish Wondra we would have to prove violations constituting contempt. This extended pressure seemed to take little account of the victims of the fraud.

The decision also further hardened the attitudes of the Corporation Counsel lawyers, who became even more resistant to our requests to advance the case. Each time we requested the Law Department to take minor action, such as to demand that Wondra disclose its list of customers, we encountered icy attitudes. "You people have mucked up the case enough already," said Tanner. "We were close to signing a consent decree but we failed because of your unreasonable demands. We'd better start thinking about proving our case with the complaints we have instead of going on a fishing expedition. We'd antagonize the court and we've already taken one beating on this case."

When I left the Department, the Wondra investigation had been pending more than a year, and Wondra's collectors were telephoning our complainants, telling them that the Department of Consumer Affairs had lost its motion, and that they had therefore better resume payments or face legal action.

Perhaps it is in the nature of bureaucracy that its members spend as much time battling each other as they devote to the mission of the institution. It may be that we were lucky to avoid serious conflict within the Department, and could reserve our strength for warfare with other city agencies. Such sentiments were small solace; we regarded the city's Law Department as a more serious threat to consumer protection than any ravaging corporation, and having weekly to beg, cajole, and outwit our own supposed advocate demoralized us for long periods.

From their perspective, it was not unreasonable to discourage us from enforcing the law. The Corporation Counsel lawyers constantly told us that they had "other pressing matters" to attend to, and they did. Some of the lawyers who were assigned to handle our cases had spent years bringing suit against persons and companies that had cheated the city out of tens of millions of dollars; consumer problems were the smallest part of their world, and they regarded as trivial the bilking of a purchaser who lost only four dollars, or even a few hundred.

Also, the city's litigating attorneys were themselves constrained by its conservative judges. Years ago, perhaps they too had been aggressive, perhaps they had even identified with the agencies they represented. Decades of appearances before judges loathe to rock the boat had taught them the folly of such a posture. The Corporation Counsel lawyers saw us as brash upstarts who would alienate the judiciary by pressing too hard and too fast.

A related fear was their apprehension that we would spoil the city's image in court by taking some risks, asking for greater relief than the judges would grant, and losing some cases. They were proud of their "win" record, and feared that the city's overall credibility in court would diminish each time the Department lost a case or a motion in a case. Of course, this philosophy was altogether inconsistent with exploring the boundaries of a new law. But testing the new law and punishing offenders were goals subordinate to safeguarding the city's "litigating reputation" which, they felt, had been carefully built up over the years. The Corporation Counsel was therefore as reluctant to permit our own lawyers to represent the Department in court as it was to pursue our cases itself.

The issue is one of the recurring themes of law enforcement. Numerous New York City agencies have, at one time or another, attempted to win the power to go to court directly rather than through the intermediary of the Law Department; rarely have they been successful. Federal Trade Commission lawyers frequently smart over the refusal of the United States Justice Department to seek judicial punishment for violations of cease and desist orders. And, of course, prosecuting attorneys serve not only as agents and advocates of the police, but as a restraining influence, an intermediary between the police and the criminal courts.

From time to time, Commissioner Myerson would ask about progress on a case. She had not had experience in law or administration, and I always felt sheepish when trying to explain the judicial or administrative nature of the delays, as if I were apologizing for my profession. She claimed to understand, and yet it must have seemed strange that our lack of progress could be better accounted for by the passivity of our friends than the skill or power of our enemies. When it became apparent that the bureaucracy was wearing the staff down to the point of ineffectiveness, she took up the cudgel and fought a single-minded battle for our independence. Feelings were strong on both sides; the issue could be resolved only by the personal decision of Mayor Lindsay. It was not an easy one for him, for he too was worried about the city's continued credibility in the courts. But ultimately he was willing to take the chance, and the Law Enforcement Division at last won the right to make its own mistakes.[6]

NOTES

1. The sales pitch which follows is an authentic excerpt from Wondra's authorized sales presentation, supplied to the Department in response to a subpoena.

2. Emphasis in original.

3. See also the *New York Times*, October 20, 1971, p. 36, col. 7: "According to the tapes (made by the Knapp Commission) the two men (a pa-

trolman and a lawyer) spoke of a number of judges pausing after each one to say if he could be "reached"—presumably bribed. All together, "five or six" judges were characterized as being reachable, and it is these the crime committee is said to be investigating."

4. "Although the defendants deny that they have committed any fraudulent or deceptive trade practices, they nonetheless have agreed to refrain from all but three of the practices which the plaintiff seeks to enjoin through a preliminary injunction. Since there is complete agreement as to these practices except for the three mentioned, the imposition of an injunction seems unduly harsh and unnecessary. Such relief is readily available if defendants are found to be violating the agreement and representations they make to the court herein. (As for the demand the salesmen identify their purpose at the outset) the nature and extent of the injury resulting from defendant's salesmen's attempts to defer announcing the true purpose of their visit during preliminary and engaging discourse has not been demonstrated. . . . The motion is denied."

5. See Schrag, "Bleak House 1968: A Report on Consumer Test Litigation," 44 N.Y.U.L. Rev. 115 (1969). The case was eventually settled, but the settlement reflected the relatively weak bargaining position of the Department. Loss of the motion, having to negotiate through unsympathetic counsel, and company pressure on complainants all contributed to this weakness.

6. This right was subject to Corporation Counsel veto on the initiation of new suits, which has never been exercised.

5 · Litigation: The Case of the Kidnapped Lawyers

As the Law Enforcement Division grew, we hired more lawyers. Eventually I noticed that the way I was describing the job to applicants was changing. I began asking candidates whether they would like to be private detectives.

The inspectors had received more complaints about Kramer's Appliance Repair Company than about any other service store in the city, and had been utterly unable to obtain any cooperation from the store's managers. The complaint of Mr. and Mrs. Homer Strong was typical.

When their television broke, Mr. and Mrs. Strong, who live in Queens, looked in the Queens Yellow Pages for a repair shop. The Kramer advertisement was one of the largest in the book, so they chose to call Kramer's, assuming that the size of the advertisement was related to the size and reputation of the company. Kramer's answered right away and immediately sent a repairman to the Strong home.

The man turned on the set and looked at the defective picture, but did not look at the back of the television. He said he would have to take the set to the shop for repair. Mr.

Strong asked that Kramer's give him an estimate of the price before performing any repairs, and the repairman agreed.[1] He left with the set.

Three days later, the store called Mrs. Strong, and said that the cost of repairs would be $74.20. She told the man not to do any repair work unless her husband called to authorize it. The following day, Mr. Strong called Kramer's to say that the price was too high and the work should not be done. The man at Kramer's said that the work had already been done, and the set was in perfect working condition. Mr. Strong felt he'd been taken, but figured there was nothing he could do, so he agreed to pay for the repairs. The man said that payment would have to be made in cash; the store did not accept personal checks, on which payment could be stopped.

When a man came to return the set, Mrs. Strong discovered that it still did not work. Neverthless, the repairman demanded payment in full, and refused to leave the set in the house unless she gave him the $74.20. She refused, and they argued for a while, finally agreeing that if Mrs. Strong paid him forty dollars in cash, he would leave the set, the balance of the money to be paid when the repairs were completed. The delivery man said the set needed only a minor adjustment, which he could do in ten minutes the next day.

He called the next night, and said he had to take the set back to the shop; the adjustment could not be made without dismantling the television. Reluctantly, the Strongs agreed to this procedure, and Kramer's said it would send a man.

They did not hear from Kramer's for a week. Then, one day, Mrs. Strong found a note in her mailbox, scribbled on a Kramer's receipt form: "Mr. Strong, it's all over. Forget you. Kramer's." Mr. Strong called Kramer's to protest, and Kramer's said it would send a man to pick up the set, which it did.

For a week, Mr. Strong called Kramer's to find out when the set would be re-delivered. He could never get an answer. Finally a woman called him to say that the set had been fixed, and that a $15.00 charge for a new transformer would be added to the bill. Mr. Strong said that he would not pay the additional charge, since Kramer's had told him that his set had already been put in perfect working condition. Kramer's refused to return the set, and Strong complained to the Department.

The inspectors discovered that Kramer's had no Queens repair shop at all. Despite its prominent advertisement in the Queens Yellow Pages, its only premises consisted of a small storefront in the Sheepshead Bay section of Brooklyn, near Coney Island.

Stephen Newman got the case, along with Bruce Ratner, another former student of mine. Newman assigned a law student to visit Kramer's and size the place up, and if necessary, to serve a subpoena. The student made an appointment to meet Mr. Sam Kramer, the owner, at the store one morning, but when he got there, the store was locked (the Yellow Pages advertisement indicated that it was open twenty-four hours a day). He telephoned the store, and Mrs. Kramer, evidently speaking from her home, answered. She said that Mr. Kramer would come right over. When he arrived, the student tried to discuss a few complaints with Kramer, but got nowhere, so as he was leaving, he served the subpoena on Kramer.

On the day of the hearing, Kramer appeared with Irving F. Raskin, an attorney. Although the hearing was scheduled to begin at 2:00, the fuses in the building blew at that hour, and the lights did not come back on until 3:00. When the questioning finally started, Raskin became obstructive, ordering his client not to answer most of the questions. For example:

> NEWMAN: How many employees do you have there?
> RASKIN: I don't want to clutter up the record with my objections; however, the purpose of this hearing and the purpose of your organization is to check into fraudulent trade practices. . . . I will ask my client not to answer these irrelevant questions. . . .
> NEWMAN: We wish to find out whether Mr. Kramer is a single employee and therefore may be having trouble with a large volume of TV sets. . . .

RASKIN: Is it your position that if he has too large a volume of work that this constitutes an unfair trade practice? . . . I deem it objectionable.

NEWMAN: Do you employ any people who repair any TV sets?

RASKIN: That is objectionable and he will not answer.

NEWMAN: . . . What percentage of your business is derived from repairs of T.V. sets?

RASKIN: Objection.

NEWMAN: Would you state your objection?

RASKIN: Objection is that these are vague, general questions which have no relevance to a fraud situation. . . .

NEWMAN: What is the average time you keep a TV in the shop for repairs?

RASKIN: Objection and may I add, it is an impossible question for any T.V. repairman to answer. It is like asking what is the average time that a legal matter stays in the attorney's office. It just cannot be answered. . . .

NEWMAN: Did you receive complaints in 1970?

RASKIN: Objection. I certainly, under no condition will allow my client to be in the position to give you information as to that, so that you can now get together a case against him. I will not put him in that position. . . . The number of complaints that Mr. Kramer had received, if any, has no relevance to this hearing.

The hearing record was a shambles. The stenographer made matters worse by announcing, in violation of the contract between her agency and the city, that she had to leave at 4:00, an hour after the hearing started. Raskin claimed then, and subsequently, in court, that the electrical breakdown and the stenographer's departure proved that the department was bent only on harassing his client.

Analyzing the record, we knew that we would have to sue Kramer's. We held a strategy meeting and decided that to bolster our case, we would rely not only on the testimony of complainants, but we'd have a customer whose set had just been repaired by Kramer's take it immediately to an honest repair company, and obtain an independent assessment. Just as our strategy meeting was concluding, an inspector came into my office. "I've got a police photographer in my office upstairs," he said, "who just got gypped terribly by an appliance repair shop."

"Don't tell me the name of the company," I said. "Let me tell you."

"Kramer's," said Bruce Ratner.

"How did you know?" said the inspector.

The policeman took his set immediately to another repair store, an authorized dealer of the company that had manufactured it. The dealer wrote to the Department that although Kramer's had charged the policeman $45.58 for the replacement or repair of two condensers, a circuit breaker, and the tuner, and for realignment, "the set had a new circuit breaker installed recently. Other than that there is no sign of anything else replaced or touched recently. The set has a covering of dust over the entire chassis and picture tube high-voltage lead. It is hardly possible to work on the under part of the chassis without leaving traces of handling somewhere on these parts. Therefore it seems to us that the set has not been taken out of the cabinet."

Meanwhile, we'd learned that Kramer was farming sets out for repair to other shops. The proprietor of one such store told us that Kramer occasionally cannibalized sets and sent them to him for repair "with the guts hanging out." This man was discontinuing his association with Kramer, because he had sets taking up space in his shop which Kramer hadn't picked up for three months. He also informed us that Kramer had been convicted of forgery in 1966, for which he'd received a three-month suspended sentence; he'd heard, too, that Kramer was currently in trouble again with the federal authorities. We contacted the postal inspectors, who told us that they suspected him of stealing checks from the mails, but said that they could not prove it.

This proprietor told us that Harry's TV also did work for Kramer, and that Max Gordon, a former benchman for Harry's, was currently a benchman for Kramer. We determined to subpoena Gordon, and since his house was near Kramer's

store, in the far reaches of Brooklyn, we decided to subpoena
Kramer again as well, and attempt to hold a more orderly
hearing than before. Newman and Ratner were despatched
to serve the subpoenas late one chilly November afternoon.

They decided to try Gordon's house first, a two-family
dwelling on a quiet Brooklyn street. Gusts of wind were blow-
ing as they approached it and they could smell the scent of
burning leaves. From across the street they could see that the
screen door to Gordon's house was closed, but the main door,
behind it, was open. Behind the screen stood a man. A child
was playing in the driveway.

They walked up to the door. "Are you Max Gordon?"
Ratner asked.

"Yes," he said, puzzled.

"We have this for you," said Ratner, extending the paper
and the two dollar witness fee.

Gordon opened the screen to see what the paper was, and
Ratner thrust it into the house.

"What's this?" Gordon asked, grabbing it.

"It's a subpoena."

"I'm not accepting this," he said, letting the papers fall to
the floor.

Newman and Ratner let the screen door close and walked
briskly away from the house. "You dropped your money."
Newman called over his shoulder. "That's your witness fee."

Pleased with themselves, and chuckling about how easy it
had been, the young lawyers began walking to the store to
serve Kramer. By the time they got there, the sky was dark
and the temperature had dropped considerably. Through
Kramer's soaped-over window, they could see a small light.
No other store on the isolated street was open. They walked
in.

The store had a small front room, which they entered.
The room was dark, and as they walked they had difficulty
avoiding bumping into televisions and chassis, which filled
the area. From the front room, a very narrow corridor led to

a back office, in which a bare bulb illuminated three men: a teen-age boy, an enormous Negro benchman, and a red-headed middle-aged man. Ratner and Newman started to walk to the office, but the men stood up and blocked them in the corridor.

"Is Mr. Kramer here?" asked Ratner.

"He's not in," said the Negro. Something in his manner suggested that he was not surprised to see the lawyers.

"Where is he?"

"Europe."

"Do you expect him back soon?"

"We don't know when he'll be back."

Suddenly, a noise at the front door caused Ratner and Newman to turn around. In walked Gordon, swinging a bunch of keys in his hand. Newman knew at once that Gordon intended to lock the door from the inside.

Newman moved forward quickly, trying to get between Gordon and the door. Gordon pushed his elbow into Newman's stomach, keeping him from the door. He locked the door, and put the keys in his pocket.

At this point Newman and Ratner abandoned their plan to serve Kramer and started to think about how they were going to get out. The four men surrounded them on all sides. The lawyers figured that they would be lucky to get away with a small beating.

Gordon said, "These are the guys I just told you about."

"Please let us out," Newman said.

"You're not going any place until I find out what this is about," said Gordon, menacingly.

"We gave you the subpoena," said Newman. "Everything is explained in there. It's all written there." He was trying desperately to avoid sounding flip. "Now please let us out."

"Who sent you?" asked Gordon.

"Philip Schrag," said my good friend Newman.

"What's his phone number?"

"I don't know. You can call him at the office in the morning. Would you let us out now please?"

"You're not getting out of here until I get his phone number and call him."

During the conversation, which lasted about fifteen minutes, Ratner had started to collect himself. He remembered that he was a lawyer as well as a prisoner. "You are keeping us here under arrest," he said. "We'll take legal action against you if you don't let us out."

"Kidnapping, eh?" Gordon laughed.

"Don't laugh," warned Ratner. "It just might be kidnapping."

"What's Schrag's phone number?"

"We don't know," said Newman.

"This is false imprisonment," said Ratner. "You'll be liable both civilly and criminally."

Gordon began to look worried. He looked around to his companions for support.

The Negro spoke. "If they gave that paper to me," he said, "I'd just put a bullet in 'em."

That made Gordon even more nervous. "Get the hell out of here," he said. He opened the door for Newman and Ratner.

A few minutes later, Gordon called me at my home. I hadn't yet heard anything from Newman and Ratner. "I'm calling you to protest, Mr. Schrag," he said. "Two fellows came to my house today and refused to identify themselves. Without saying a word, they threw a subpoena at me and ran away. Is that any way to behave?"

I took his number and told him I'd call him back.

After a while, I reached Ratner and learned what actually had happened. I called Gordon at his home, and his wife said he was at Kramer's. Then I called Kramer's and asked for Gordon.

"He's not in," said a voice.

"Put him on," I said.

"There's no one here by that name," protested the voice.

"I know he's there. Put him on." I tried to sound tough.

Gordon came to the phone. "Mr. Gordon," I said, "when

you called me a little while ago, you neglected to tell me something."

"What's that?"

"That you imprisoned two officials of the Department of Consumer Affairs."

There was a pause. "Well, I wasn't the one who locked the door."

"I think you were," I said. "And I don't care if you weren't. You are going to sit down immediately and write letters of apology to Mr. Newman and Mr. Ratner, and you are going to come to a hearing on the return date of your subpoena."

"What if I don't show up?" he asked.

"Then we'll punish you," I said.

"What if I'm sick?"

"We'll still punish you."

The next day, Ratner and Newman received exquisitely hedged letters from Gordon, handwritten on a page from a yellow pad:

Dear Mr. Newman:

I cannot tell you how embarrassed and ashamed I am at the incident which occurred on November 19, 1970. I was terribly upset at the time and lost control. I wish to offer my sincere apologies at this time.

Yours truly,
Max Gordon

On the day of the hearing, Gordon appeared, represented by Raskin. Once again Raskin was obstructive, and no useful information was developed. However, Newman could sense that Gordon didn't really know anything, so rather than apply for a court order compelling Gordon to answer the questions, Newman decided that somehow he would eventually serve Kramer again, and make a record for an order compelling Kramer to answer.

More complaints about Kramer's continued to come in. One lady wrote that Mr. Kramer told her that his prices were lower than those of his competitors because "I over-charge niggers in Harlem 30% to 50%. They're unreliable so they don't deserve better."

We began to compile papers for a lawsuit. We decided we needed more expert testimony; we wanted to take no chances that we'd lose a case against Kramer. RCA generously made available to the Department a television set and the services of an expert technician, who caused the set to break by burning out a single resistor. We placed this set in an investigator's home; Kramer's man looked at the set and took it to the shop to be fixed. Five days later he returned it, for which the investigator had to pay $41.35 cash. She demanded an itemized receipt; it showed replacement or repair of three resistors, three condensers, and the tuner, as well as realignment. Our RCA technician determined that only the burnt-out resistor had been touched.

We also asked the municipal television station, WNYC-TV, for help. That time we went all out. Its expert gave a set a complete examination, and found it to be in perfect condition. He then inserted a single defective tube; a competent repairman could have fixed it in the owner's home. He painted the inside components of the set with invisible ink, and we put the television in another investigator's home. Kramer's came, and said the set had to be taken to the shop, because there was a "short in the transformer." They returned it for payment of $56.20, with an itemized statement that they had replaced a tube, cleaned a condenser, and aligned and cleaned the tuner. The WNYC-TV technician found that such work was neither necessary nor performed.

Up to this point, we had not attempted to discuss individual complaints with Kramer. But we had one low-income complainant for whom the cost of repair represented a major burden, and who wanted us to try to do something for her immediately. Ratner called Kramer to discuss this case. Kramer was civil for a few minutes, but he refused to return the woman's television before she paid for it, or even to let her test the set, to see that it was working, before she handed over her payment.

"That's unreasonable, Mr. Kramer," Ratner pleaded.

"O.K. Ratner, I've had it," said Kramer. "Now you're going to hear the real me. What do you want me to do? Kill Mayor Lindsay? Fuck Mayor Lindsay! Fuck Bess Myerson. Fuck your whole Department. . . ." This went on for about a minute, and then Kramer slammed down the telephone.

We advised the complaining woman, and several others, to sue Kramer's in Small Claims Court. The summons, in that court, is served by registered mail, sent by the court clerk. In Kramer's case, however, the envelopes from the clerk to Kramer, which had the name of the court printed as a return address, were returned to the clerk unclaimed; Kramer had simply refused them. The clerk then advised the consumers to serve the summonses on Kramer themselves, but no one wanted to venture to the far reaches of Brooklyn. We collected together a small brigade of Kramer complainants, and one of them volunteered to go out and serve all of the Small Claims summonses. He had no trouble serving Kramer at the store. But Kramer did not appear in Small Claims Court.

The customers, therefore, won judgments against Kramer's by default. But the judgments were hollow victories; Kramer refused to pay them the money they were entitled to. The customers then called city marshals, whose job it is to collect judgments for a fee. The customers tried various marshals, and in each case the marshal's secretary took down the facts of the matter in shorthand. But when she heard that the amount involved was under one hundred dollars—which meant that the fee would be very small—she said that the marshal was out of town and she didn't know when he'd be back. The customers finally tried to employ the sheriff, who is authorized to levy on bank accounts to collect judgments, but he could not locate any bank account for Kramer.

At this time, the 1971 Queens Yellow Pages were published. The first ad we looked up was Kramer's. We were astonished. This year, Kramer's advertisement listed addresses for four Queens locations. We were pretty sure his only store was in Sheepshead Bay, so we checked the Queens addresses. One was an empty storefront, one a town house, one a vacant lot, and one an intersection with no television repair shop.

Commissioner Myerson wrote to the President of the telephone company, reciting not only the fraud in the Yellow Pages, but Kramer's activities generally. He designated company Vice-President Walter Bohn, to meet with us. In an exploratory switch to the "direct action" strategy, we asked Mr. Bohn to prevent deception through the Yellow Pages by changing Kramer's telephone number, and not putting a recording on the old number informing customers of the new number. In other words, the telephone company could neutralize its own false advertisement by rendering the listed number inoperable, without depriving Kramer's of service altogether.

Bohn was unwilling to do this. Although the telephone company did not condone falsehood, he told us, it could not legally discriminate against a user. We pointed out that punishing a fraudulent advertiser was hardly discrimination, but he said that the company could only insist that Kramer's future advertising be true.

We proposed several alternative suggestions: putting a tape recording on Kramer's number that would tell customers that the advertisement was false before ringing at Kramer's store; printing a notice in Kramer's advertisement in the Brooklyn Yellow Pages, about to be published, that Kramer's Queens Yellow Pages advertising was false, and printing a full-page notice on the inside cover of all future Yellow Pages, warning consumers that the advertising in the book might be fraudulent, and should not necessarily be believed. Bohn rejected each suggestion.

We then told him that if the telephone company refused to do anything to correct false advertising it had published, and refused to warn the public that Yellow Pages advertising was unreliable, Commissioner Myerson might have to warn the public about the Yellow Pages herself, in a press conference. Suddenly Mr. Bohn said that he would pass the case along to higher company officials who would have to decide whether to take punitive action against Kramer's.

Bohn called soon afterwards to tell me that the telephone company agreed that action should be taken; it would disconnect Kramer's number and substitute a new one, as we'd originally asked. But later the same day, he informed me that when he'd told this to Kramer, Kramer said he'd sue the telephone company, and as a matter of courtesy, the telephone company was giving him a week to draft his legal papers.

Although the Department of Consumer Affairs was not a party to the suit, Bohn kept us informed and invited us to observe. Kramer asked for a preliminary injunction against the telephone company, and the judge requested that the attorneys for the parties confer in his chambers with his law clerk.

At this meeting, Kramer was represented not by Raskin but by Ira Borden, a Manhattan Democratic District Leader.[2] The other participants were the judge's law clerk, the telephone company lawyer, and Stephen Newman.

The telephone company quickly copped out. Instead of supporting its threatened action to change the telephone number, the telephone company lawyer quickly agreed with Borden that it didn't really want to act against Kramer's, but that the Department of Consumer Affairs was forcing it to. The law clerk, a quiet gentleman of about forty-five, was instinctively hostile to the Department—which was cast in the role of an instigator—so Newman found himself isolated. All of the clerk's questions were hostile, and all were directed at him. After hearing Newman, the clerk told him that the proper way to proceed would be to commence the Department's own suit against Kramer's and ask for an immediate injunction. Newman said that we were preparing to do that, but we had no illusions that we could get the other side to agree to a quick submission to the court.

The law clerk left the room for a while; when he returned, he said he had discussed the case with the chief clerk, who had said that the Department was acting in a totalitarian manner.

The court's decision was predictable, in view of the law clerk's beliefs. The telephone company was enjoined from changing Kramer's number because, assuming that the charge of false advertising in the Yellow Pages was true, changing the telephone number was "disproportionate" to the harm done by Kramer.[3]

Our only remaining course of action was to take the traditional route—sue Kramer's. By this time we had the power to bring our own lawsuits, and had put the papers together. On April 16, 1971, we obtained a court order permitting us to expedite the proceedings by commencing the suit immediately and having our motion for a preliminary injunction heard three days later, on April 19. There was just one hitch: the order had to be served on Kramer, himself, personally, that very day. Naturally, I assigned the job of serving process on Kramer to two experts—Newman and Ratner.

They drove to Brooklyn, taking with them their secretary, Gano Stephens, in case getting into Kramer's presence required a female to participate in a ruse. The trio reached the store late in the afternoon; it was locked, and no one appeared to be inside. Newman decided to try Kramer's home, in a nearby apartment complex.

Ratner and Stephens rang the doorbell of Kramer's apartment. A woman, evidently Kramer's wife, answered. Gano Stephens introduced herself. "I'm Jean Maller," she said. "My husband and I"—she indicated Bruce Ratner—"live downstairs. We've heard that the landlord is thinking of making the building a cooperative, and we wanted to find out what our neighbors in the building think of it."

Mrs. Kramer, delighted to hear that the building might be co-op'd, let them in.

"Is your husband in?" asked Ratner.

"No, he's not."

"Can you tell us when he'll be back?" asked Stephens. "We want to get the reactions of both adults in the family."

The telephone rang, and Mrs. Kramer answered it. "Kramer's Appliance Repair!" she said. There was a pause. Mrs. Kramer continued, "Just shut up," she told the caller. "You got your television back in good condition. Now stop complaining."

Another call came through just as she hung up. "Cash or no set," she told the customer.

Ratner and Stephens stretched out the visit as long as they could, hoping that Kramer would come home. It became difficult to invent any further questions regarding Mrs. Kramer's feelings about buying a cooperative apartment. Fortunately, Mrs. Kramer kept interrupting to take telephone calls for Kramer's. Ratner noticed also that she had a red telephone which was an open line to the store.

Finally Ratner and Stephens left, and rejoined Newman who'd been waiting outside. Night had fallen; the papers had to be served within a few hours. Feeling quite depressed over their failure to serve Kramer, the group drove to a nearby McDonald's for a hamburger.

After dinner, they drove back to Kramer's. Now a light was on inside; it might be Kramer. But they suspected that if they knocked, no one would open the door, and even if the door were opened, they would never get to Kramer. Furthermore, they had seen enough of the inside of that store under similar conditions.

They went to a telephone booth in a bar across the street and dialed 911, the police emergency number. They had no idea whether the police would help them, or whether legally the police could do so, but they had nothing to lose. After they explained their mission, the precinct sergeant said that he would send a squad car to meet them outside of Kramer's.

While they were waiting for the car, another squad car drove by, and they flagged it down, just as the first car arrived. Both cars pulled up in front of Kramer's, their red lights flashing in the darkness. One policeman walked to the door with Newman. The lawyers' depression had been replaced by a feeling that all would go well. Newman knocked.

"Who is it," growled a voice. It sounded like Kramer.

"The police," said the cop.

Kramer opened a crack in the frosted-over door. He could see only the policeman, not Newman who was standing to one side. "Mr. Kramer?" asked the cop.

"Yes . . ."

"These gentlemen have some legal papers to serve upon you."

Newman stepped into Kramer's line of vision, and extended the papers. A disgusted expression captured Kramer's features. He started to slam the door. Newman moved even more quickly, hurling the legal papers at Kramer, so that they were swept in by the closing portal.

Kramer opened the door again and kicked the court order towards the street. The papers hit the policeman in the shin.

"Now look here, Mr. Kramer," said the cop. "You've been served with legal papers. You are required to take them. Now . . . pick . . . them . . . up!"

Kramer bent down, picked up the papers, and disappeared into the store. Newman and Ratner fell over themselves thanking the policemen.

Two days later, NBC-TV carried a news story on the commencement of this suit. An anonymous neighbor of Kramer's store called NBC to say that immediately after the broadcast he saw three men carting boxes of books and records away from the shop.

The motion was supposed to be heard in three days. I expected Kramer's lawyer to ask me for a postponement, and I knew that if I said no, the court would give him at least one anyway; it is virtually impossible to get a New York judge to deny adjournments. So I determined that if he asked for a postponement I would grant it, provided he promised not to request another. Sure enough, Borden called and we agreed to put the case off for one week; Borden agreed that he would not ask again unless there were a genuine emergency.

A week passed. The night before we were to go to court, Borden requested a second one-week postponement. He said he had been sick. I did what is never done among New York practitioners: I refused.

He went to court and asked the judge to give him another week. I explained the urgency of the case, and the fact that Borden had had an extra week already, but the judge said, "The man says he's been sick. A man is entitled to one adjournment so I'll give him a week, but I'll mark on the record that there can be no more adjournments." [4]

Two days before the case was to be heard, Borden called me. "Sorry, Schrag," he said. "I'm withdrawing from the case. I can't get Kramer to pay me the fee he owes me."

And the next day, I received a call from . . . Irving Raskin. "I've just been retained by Kramer's," he said. "I need at least a week to familiarize myself with the case."

"Familiarize?" I asked. "You've been on this case from the beginning. You represented Kramer at a hearing months ago."

"A lot has happened since then," he said, truthfully.

"The answer is no," I said. "The judge has marked the record, 'No more adjournments.' "

He applied to the court. "A lawyer can't serve his client unless he has time to familiarize himself with the case," the judge lectured me. Another week's delay was granted.

We thought we had an open-and-shut case. We'd filed numerous affidavits from complaining consumers, as well as experts' affidavits in the three instances in which we'd arranged for technicians to analyze the work Kramer's did. When the delays finally came to an end, we were most anxious to see how Kramer would reply.

His response was amazing. He noted that the Department supported a bill to license repair shops, but no legislative action had yet been taken. "What the plaintiff is attempting to do by judicial authority it has failed to do by legislative enactment as of this date. It is highly discriminatory to set up a set of rules for the defendant as the only licensed TV repair man and the remainder of the industry to continue [sic] to operate without any regulations at all." Kramer said that the telephone company had insisted that he put some address in his Yellow Pages advertising and that when he said he had no Queens address to put in that borough's telephone book, the telephone company salesman had advised him to do what other companies did—make up a few.

Kramer denied he cheated people. He said he had a large business, and some people were bound to be disgruntled. "I can name a number of people who are quite satisfied and have congratulated and thanked the defendant for its service, and such people as are included are the Republican National Committee, Federal Reserve Bank of New York, IBM Company, New York Telephone Company, Democratic Party, Paul O'Dwyer, Mayor Lindsay."

Kramer dismissed the expert technicians by saying that these were "plants," not "actual consumers." "The court should merely bear in mind this is one of those 'entrapment situations.' "

A few weeks later, the court rendered its decision, and again we lost. The judge noted that Kramer's admitted that the advertising was false. This did not matter, because according to the court, "many efficient and honest repair businesses in various fields of endeavor have only one central repair shop that services the entire city." Furthermore, we'd presented evidence with respect to only a small percentage of Kramer's customers; perhaps they represented the freak case rather than the norm. We could not have an injunction to prevent misconduct, but the judge did give us a ray of hope: we could ask again if Kramer's refused to submit to trial in ten days.[5]

The decision angered and depressed us, but we were determined to give the judicial system every opportunity to demonstrate that it was capable of rendering some kind of justice. We served Kramer's lawyer with a demand for a trial in ten days. We suspected that the move was fruitless, even if Kramer's consented; we understood that there was at least a six-month backlog for trials, and that the court clerks would not take a case out of turn unless a judge ordered it. Our judge had merely invited us to apply for such an order if the other side agreed; he had not set a trial date.

The problem did not arise, however, because Kramer's lawyer refused to consent. So we availed ourselves of the right which the court had given us to ask again for a preliminary injunction. This time we expected a better response, because Kramer was being obviously obstructive. Also, we were encouraged because this time, the court clearly faced an all-or-nothing decision; the last day for trials before the three-month summer recess had now passed.

Yet we lost once again, this time because by offering only ten days, we were not giving Kramer's enough time to prepare a proper defense.[6] The court ordered Kramer's to be ready for a trial on the first trial date after the court's recess.

But in mid-summer, Raskin notified the Department that he wished to take Commissioner Myerson's deposition; that is, to examine her under oath before trial. The Department felt constrained to resist; permitting what it regarded as unwarranted harassment of the Commissioner would have set a bad administrative precedent. It therefore decided to resist the demand in court, but litigation over the propriety of the proposed deposition had to precede the trial. The judge's order setting a trial date was automatically nullified and the trial postponed indefinitely.

When I left the Department, the investigation was more than a year old. The Department's lawyers were still sparring with Raskin. Consumers were calling with new complaints about Kramer's; the Department's lawyers had to say that they were sorry, but there was nothing they could do. The complainants could not understand why a city agency supported by their tax dollars could not help them.

And Kramer's still had Mr. Strong's television.

We had always regarded the Kramer's case as one of the strongest in the office. The evidence was clear; not only did we have a concededly false Yellow Pages advertisement and a substantial number of complaints from consumers, but we had gone to great expense, relative to our small budget, to obtain expert analyses of Kramer's work in relation to the store's promises, and in three out of three cases checked by technicians, Kramer had lied about the work performed. Furthermore, because Kramer's was still holding our complainants' televisions after months of Departmental complaint investigation, the equities seemed strong for judicial intervention. Our confidence in the power of our evidence was matched only by our incredulity at the unwillingness of the court to act on it.

Most of the lawyers in the Department had just graduated from law school. Cases like Kramer's were their first exposure to the behavior of courts. They were surprised that the first Kramer's decision was made, for all practical purposes, not by a judge but by a law clerk who had been instinctively hostile to our position. But that decision, at least, might be justifiable since we were asking a public utility to take on a new, debatable responsibility to prevent fraud by one of its subscribers.

The lawyers were puzzled by the second decision. To them, the fact that it was possible to operate an honest city-wide repair service with only a single location did not lead logically to the court's proposition that the admission of false advertising by a dishonest company should not prompt judicial action. And if the court was not persuaded by the Department's experience with expert testers and by the testimony of the technicians, how were we supposed to prove that a company regularly violated the law? Theoretically, it might be possible to commission a statistically valid opinion survey of a representative sample of a company's customers, but their names and addresses were almost always withheld from us, and even if we had the names, the cost of the survey, at the going rate of approximately fifty dollars an interview, would have been enormous. Furthermore, if we had taken a survey and could demonstrate that a company cheated 5% of

its customers, would that galvanize a court into action? Five
per cent could represent a substantial number of people, but
the court seemed concerned not with numbers but with proportion. How often did a company have to steal before a
court would tell it to behave?

The third decision was the one that radicalized the young
lawyers. They had been cursed at, held captive, delayed and
defeated in court, but finally they had procured a probably
meaningless order entitling them to a trial in ten days. They
informed the company of their readiness to present the evidence in court, and the company mocked them. Yet when
they returned to court, the same judge who had set down the
"ten-day" rule characterized their desire to have a trial after
that time as failure to give the defendant "at least a minimum period of time to prepare a proper defense." And the
second trial date set by the court proved equally illusory.

Between the second and the third Kramer decision, Deputy Commissioner Henry Stern and I visited the judge on
other business; we wanted to explore the possibility of spon-
soring a seminar for the judges, to educate them about our
problems in presenting our cases to the courts and obtaining
judicial sympathy. This judge had known Stern for years,
and the meeting was very cordial. He asked us for an example of what we considered lack of sympathy from the judiciary; since his involvement with the Kramer case appeared to
be over (we did not know that the renewed application for an
injunction would be assigned to him), we described what
happened in that instance.

"Everyone comes into this court wanting an immediate
injunction," he said. "But I've been here a long time and I've
discovered that there's practically no case that can't wait
until the day after tomorrow. Injunctions are harsh remedies.
They should only be granted sparingly."

I pointed out that because of the clogged court calendars,
parties had to wait many months to get trials. Preliminary
injunctions were often the whole ball game, because a company could cheat thousands of people while the Department

was waiting for a trial, and could even then go out of business.

He gave us a lecture that lasted ten or fifteen minutes. He knew that even if he ordered an immediate trial, he said, the calendars were so backlogged that we couldn't get one for six months. But that was *our* fault, not his. *We* worked for the city of New York, and it was the city that would not give the court sufficient funds to hire enough secretaries or clerks. He observed, correctly, that the country claims to believe in law and order, but its appropriations to courts and its acquiescence in tremendous court backlogs proved otherwise. Things would get worse before they got better, he warned, and that was the fault of the politicians, not the judges. "This country hasn't had any moral leadership since the Kennedys were shot," he added.

We were stunned. In large measure, the judge was right. Our problems stemmed not so much from judicial reluctance to grant relief on the basis of sterile papers rather than trials, but that the machinery of justice, including trials, had broken down, and nobody cared. He indicated the window. "There are felons out there going free because the political leadership won't provide money for police, prosecutors, defense counsel, courts, jails, rehabilitation, or even for the prevention of crime or the control of narcotics. You think you have problems? If we ever do get more money to fund this court, I hope we put it into crime control. Sure consumer fraud should be eliminated. But we're short of resources and it's not the priority area."

We often brooded about the judge's sentiments. We all lived in the city of New York, so it was obvious that there were more pressing problems than consumer fraud, including not only the high crime rate but the deteriorating schools, the housing shortage, and more than anything else, the tendency toward compartmentalization of the inner city into pockets for an increasingly wealthy white middle class among an increasingly alienated, poor, black population. Should young lawyers devote their resources to fighting consumer fraud, when so many worse things were happening?[7] Doubt about the priority to be given the elimination of consumer fraud mingled with the depressing awareness that law enforcement of any type was inevitably a negative activity. The people we were fighting were making, fixing, or at least distributing things. They acted, and appeared to be producing something tangible. We reacted, always to stop something, never to create it.

Staff demoralization was always cured by client contact. The frustration of dealing with Enchanting, Wondra, and Kramer's upset our lawyers, but those frustrations nearly drove some consumers insane. We talked to customers who had called Kramer's thirty or forty times, pleading for the return of a television that was one of their few links with the world; they had been insulted and abused, and that experience, no less than crime in the streets or drugs in the schools had increased their fury at urban society. We went on fighting consumer fraud not, as the common wisdom would have it, to make the country safe for "legitimate business" and the sale of even more unnecessary products, but to punish vicious men who robbed, not one victim at a time at the end of a dark alley, but thousands of persons at the end of a mail order plan, franchising scheme, door-to-door selling swindle, or mass media advertisement.

But cases such as Kramer's led to increasing cynicism about how effective we could be by working through bureaucratic and judicial channels. Our frustration and occasional rage led us to explore new strategies, to discard some of the self-imposed restraints on tactics. Gradually, our methods of investigation became less gentlemanly, and our bite more ferocious.

NOTES

1. In most cases, the repairman told our complainants that they would charge four dollars for giving an estimate, to which the customers readily agreed.

2. Politically connected lawyers often represented the companies we were fighting. In the space of a few months, for example, we squared off against not only this District Leader, but a former Regional Commissioner of the Department of Housing and Urban Development, a former Counsel to Mayor Lindsay, a defeated candidate for Governor of New York, and a defeated candidate for United States Senator.

3. "Motion for a temporary injunction is granted. It is undenied and clear that plaintiff's business is substantially dependent upon business received over the telephone. . . . The basis for the threatened action is defendant's receipt of advice that the various addresses listed by plaintiff as its warehouses in its advertisements in the classified directories are not in fact plaintiff's warehouses. [Assuming this charge is true,] the action threatened is disproportionate to the wrong asserted. Other remedies are available including correction of the advertisement, not the substantially complete elimination of the prime source of plaintiff's business."

4. The judge may have meant that a man is morally entitled to delay; no such right appears in the statute books.

5. "Briefly stated, defendants are charged with an unlawful scheme designed to force their customers to pay high bills for television repairs which defendants falsely claim to have performed. A temporary injunction is an extraordinary remedy, which is sparingly granted upon a showing of a clear right to relief and the threat of irreparable injury. Moreover, the sweeping injunction . . . which plaintiff seeks, in effect, determines the litigation and gives substantially the same relief that could be obtained by a final judgment after trial. Such preliminary injunctions should be granted only when necessity requires it.

"Although defendants admit that they have falsely advertised in the . . . telephone directory, this fact is insufficient in itself to prompt a temporary injunction since many efficient and honest repair businesses in various fields of endeavor have only one central repair shop that services the entire City. Moreover, it is uncontested that defendants' encompasses repairs to thousands of television sets each year. This court is quite hesitant at this time to pass final judgment upon an entire enterprise on the basis of the purported treatment of a small percentage of its customers [and defendants deny that they cheated the customers who filed affidavits]. Accordingly, the motion for a temporary injunction is denied without prejudice to renewal thereof in the event that the defendants shall fail to consent to an immediate trial of the action upon ten days notice by the plaintiff of her readiness to go to trial."

6. "Defendants refused to consent to immediate trial and, hence, the instant motion was brought. Upon renewal, a perusal of the moving affidavit fails to reveal any new evidentiary matter that might now induce the court to grant the drastic relief that has been previously denied. . . . Although the public interest demands that the serious allegations of wrongdoing herein be resolved at the earliest possible date, the interests of justice also require that the defendant be given at least a minimum period of time to prepare a proper defense. . . . [The new motion is denied and]

the present action is given a trial preference and the parties are further ordered to be ready for trial on the first day in September of 1971."

7. Another judge I know always asks me, "Are you still doing that consumer fraud stuff? When are you going to join the class struggle?" He's kidding, but not completely.

6 · Pressure: The Case of the Purloined Pitch

PERHAPS NO CONSUMER FRAUD has affected as many people in urban areas in recent years as the magazine subscription gyps. The Department received dozens of complaints from people who had signed "PDS" or "paid-during-service" magazine subscription contracts.

The customers had been telephoned at their homes or offices and told that the caller was conducting a survey of reading habits. What magazines, the caller wanted to know, do you read on a trip? The caller suggested some well-known, national magazines, and the resident gave his comments. For his cooperation, the resident would receive five-year subscriptions to six major magazines, including the ones he'd spoken well of, at the company's expense. All he had to do was pay a small "publisher's service charge which is only sixty-four cents a week." Many people who received such a call laughed and hung up. Many others thought they were lucky, or privileged, to have been called; they said they were interested, and a salesman quickly appeared at their home to sign them up on a contract obligating them to pay $150 in monthly payments over two and a half years.

When they discovered that they didn't have time to read six magazines, and that the "small publisher's service charge" was the total of the regular subscription rates to the magazines, many people stopped paying. They then received a paper reading, in bold print:

48 HOUR NOTICE
FINAL NOTICE OF COURT ACTION

Final notice of court action. 48 hours from hereof our lawyers will file proceedings against you without further notice, because you have failed or neglected to comply with our request for payment. Cost of legal action, to you, court costs as much as $50.00 [sic]. THIS AMOUNT MAY BE ADDED TO YOUR ACCOUNT UNLESS YOU COMPLY WITH THE ABOVE 48-HOUR NOTICE. . . . Then an Officer of the Court may seize your goods, attach your wages, bank account or other property. He may also be instructed to bring you and your family into Court and force you and them to tell under oath what property you own. This will be embarrassing to you. . . . IT'S IMPOSSIBLE TO ESCAPE A JUDGMENT.

Although many people who received such notices thought they'd been cheated, they were terrified of court, so they paid their bills.

The Department received many complaints about Standard Magazine Service, one of the companies engaging in this type of selling. Attorney Marjorie Smith went to work on the case.

She started by looking into Standard's certificate of incorporation, and was surprised to discover that sales in New York were made by Standard Magazine Service of New York, Inc., a local franchisee of Standard Magazine Service, Inc., which was a Delaware corporation headquartered in Kansas. The Kansas company was, in turn, a wholly owned subsidiary of Transworld Publishing, Incorporated, the famous national corporation.[1]

Since the parent company and its subsidiary (but not necessarily the local franchisee) were reputable, a subpoena was not necessary to produce the presence of a Vice-President for a hearing. He came upon request, represented by an attorney who flew from Kansas. We asked him to bring several documents with him. Although he brought some of them, he claimed that certain crucial ones, such as the authorized sales pitch, were under the control of the local franchisee, not the Kansas company. He claimed to know very little about what happened on the local level; but he did know that the Kansas company had authorized the local company, and dozens like it, to sell magazines, for which the Kansas company received a percentage of the gross.

One of our investigators then paid a visit to the local office of the franchisee. The woman in charge of the office, Hilda Somers, explained her version of how she conducted her business, but she was unwilling to testify under oath or to supply business records. So we served her with the usual subpoena.

On the day she was required to testify, she failed to appear; once again we lost the twenty dollar stenographer's fee. We called her and asked why she had not come in, and she replied that her attorneys told her not to talk to us at all.

Mrs. Smith followed the call with a letter to Miss Somers, advising her that we would go to court in five days if she did not contact us. She didn't, and we did. Although we drafted the papers and applied to the court for an order in November, Miss Somers' attorneys engaged in the usual delaying tactics, so that actually, a hearing was not held for months.[2]

One night, while our application to enforce the subpoena was moving slowly through the court, Stephen Newman's telephone rang. It was Standard, which had picked his name from the telephone book as a routine victim. He made an accurate transcription of the sales pitch, and discovered that the lies contained in it were more blatant than any reported by our complainants. Evidently, their memories had acted to screen out the worst abuses, to order the world in the direction of honesty and fair dealing, even though they were complaining of being gypped.

When Mrs. Smith went over Newman's transcription, she concluded that Somers would never admit to using such a sales pitch, even if ordered to do so by the court. She decided that it would be helpful if we could get independent, irrefutable proof of the pitch used. Assuming that we could physically get away with it, would it be unethical, we wondered, to have one of our lawyers or investigators get a job with Standard, so that he or she would have access to all of the pitches?

We debated the ethical question for some time. There seemed no clear answer. What decided the question was the batting average we had earned to date playing by the rules. We decided to do it.

An investigator was assigned to apply for a job as a telephone solicitor. Standard, it developed, had a rapid employee turnover; the workers could not stomach it for long. Our investigator was easily hired, and, cassette recorder in pocketbook, she went to work for the company.

She recorded the sales presentation, and it matched what Newman had heard. Still, Mrs. Smith was not satisfied. A recording was not as good as the printed word, it would not be as convincing. We decided to photograph the printed pitch from which Standard's telephone girls read.

Marjorie McDiarmid, it developed, was a pretty serious amateur photographer. We decided to try an approach that would not involve us again in having to obtain employment. One afternoon, she and I went to the midtown office of the franchisee and knocked on the door. She wore dark glasses so that if we failed, she would have another chance. A small camera was buried in her shoulder bag.

Hilda Somers answered the door. I opened a little case and, for the first and only time during my career, flashed the brass badge bearing the city seal that identified me as the Consumer Advocate. "We're from the Department of Consumer Affairs on a routine inspection," I droned, trying to sound like this was my eighteenth such visit of the day. "May we come in?"

"No," she said. "No one comes in here. Now get out."

Thus I learned the power of a badge.

McDiarmid went back the next day, without the dark glasses, and got a job. The walls of the room in which she was to work were lined with semi-private booths; each booth had partitions on the sides, so the girls making calls could not talk to their neighbors, but was open in back, so that a supervisor in the center of the room could observe each girl working. Each booth had a chair and a flat writing surface projecting from the forward wall, on which lay a telephone, and tacked to the front wall, above the phone, was a copy of the official sales pitch.

Nervously, McDiarmid sat down and began making calls, trying to subtly affect her voice so that the person she was talking to would not really be convinced to buy magazines. She had to be careful, though, because she could be observed from behind, and she could not rule out the possibility that a company supervisor also listened in on the calls.

She felt the weight of the camera hidden in her bag. How could she remove it and use it, with someone watching behind her?

She called the supervisor over. "This copy of the presentation is too scratched up," she told her. "I'm having trouble reading from it." The supervisor removed it and posted a new, more legible copy, placing the old copy on the desk in front of McDiarmid.

A few minutes later, while speaking to a potential customer, McDiarmid folded the old copy and slipped it into a pile of scrap paper. As she did this, she didn't look around; that might arouse the suspicion of the others in the room. She couldn't know whether anyone was watching her move the papers.

Later, she furtively removed the camera from her pocketbook, and carefully placed it on her lap. She dared not put the viewfinder to her eye, for fear of being spotted, so she estimated the distance from the lens to the wall. Just as she was about to shoot a picture, a man walked into the room. She bent forward, shielding the camera with her body. The man began to talk to another girl.

Her shutter clicked.

McDiarmid slid the camera back into her pocketbook. Just to make sure, she took the scrap papers and the old copy of the pitch with her when she left.

Shortly afterwards, we won a court order requiring Miss Somers to testify. Before the hearing, Marjorie Smith xeroxed the sales pitch that McDiarmid had taken; Smith feared that Somers would snatch the original from her hands and tear it up. During the questioning, Smith asked Somers to show her a copy of the authorized sales pitch, a document that had been included in the subpoena and court order. Somers showed her a paper with this message:

Hello, Mrs. ———. Well, fine, how are you today? This is ——— from the downtown office of Standard Magazines. If you'll take a moment to answer a question, I believe I have something here that will interest you, too. Have you lived here over 3 months? You have—wonderful! Like I said, we do have something for you and with NO catches for a change. Through the facilities of our home office, we have been asked to find out if you are a permanent resident, and since you are, you can receive the next 60 issues of the fascinating Holiday, Look, Sport and Esquire (Women: Holiday, Look, McCalls and Ladies' Home Journal) all for pennies a week. Now I know you're wondering why we're doing this, or in other words, what's the catch, right? Well, there is no catch!! This is done to increase circulation. The more circulation we have, the more the advertiser is willing to place the ad. And, all we ask of you is to furnish the small subscription cost of ——— cents a week for all of them. That's all there is to it. There are no other charges and I'm sure you feel as everyone else has that this is certainly worth ——— cents a week. Don't you agree? The best part is the magazines will be mailed directly to your home and you can mail in the change monthly. We will even provide pre-addressed envelopes for you. Now just give me your correct address, the way you want them delivered and someone will stop by and leave off your contract and guarantee in a day or so. What is your address? . . . Oh, by the way, I was wondering if you could do me a personal favor. You see, my pay increase depends on how well I sell people their orders, so when the manager drops off your contract and guarantee, I was wondering if you could put in a good word for me? Thank you, my name is ————.

This pitch was misleading, but not nearly as misleading as the one that McDiarmid had photographed and taken. Smith began a series of questions designed to determine whether Somers would admit to the sales pitch her employees really used:

Q. How long has this particular sales presentation been in use?
A. Oh, a couple of years now.
Q. This is the only one that has been used by your office?
A. Variations of it.
Q. How much of a variation?
A. Not much.
Q. Do you have any copies of the variations?
A. No, I don't.
Q. How would they be used if there were variations? Would they have been printed up at one time?
A. They might have been printed up at one time.
Q. Has this been the exclusive sales presentation for any length of time?
A. We have used variations of it, but mainly that one that you have in your hand right now.
Q. Can you give me a date, the last time a variation was used?
A. I'd say a variation is a variation of maybe the sequence. It could have been used a year ago, six months ago.
Q. So that basically, aside from very slight differences, this is the only one that has been used?
A. Basically.
Q. Okay. I would like to get some idea. You keep saying "basically."

A. This is the basic presentation that we use.

Q. Well, can you remember any of the differences in the ones you say are a slight variation of this?

A. As I say, you might just change a paragraph a bit, that's about all. For example, we no longer use the term "average cost" . . . [which had been scratched out on the paper she'd given Mrs. Smith].

Q. Are there any other changes on what's currently being used on this one?

A. We use the term "contract" instead of "order slip" [another substitution that had been made in pen on the slip she'd given Mrs. Smith]. . . .

The time had come, Smith decided, to play her hand. She took from an envelope a copy of the pitch that McDiarmid had taken and showed it to Somers.

Q. O.K. Can you tell me whether you are familiar with this as a sales presentation that's ever been used by your office?

Smith laid the real sales presentation on the table:

Good afternoon. This is Miss ———— with the Standard Business Information Office and we are taking an inquiry on reading habits. If you were on a trip and a hostess came up with your choice of publications, which three would you be most likely to leaf through along the way? For your first choice would you prefer American or Esquire? Your second choice would be Ladies' Home Journal or McCalls? Your third choice: Redbook or Modern Photography? Fine. For your cooperation and to promote industry this year we will send you copies of (the three choices) along with Look, Cue and the Saturday Review, for the next sixty months, at our expense. All we do today is list your name and address. Your first name is? And your last name? And your correct business address? The name of the firm? I guess you're kind of curious as to why we're doing this. Every year we send out thousands of copies to business people like yourself in order to increase our circulation. You really get these because of our increased demand for quality circulation. All they ask you to do is to merely take care of a small publisher's service charge which is only 64 cents a week. That certainly is fair enough, isn't it? Thanks and do enjoy your magazines.

Miss Somers looked stunned. She didn't know what to say, whether to admit using this pitch, since she'd been caught, which would amount to an admission that she had just lied under oath, or to deny it and be drawn in further. There was a long pause. A minute passed.

A. Yes.
Q. When would you say that this was used?
A. It could have been used in the past year.
Q. Can you describe how that differs from the one that you handed me?
A. It's basically the same.
Q. So that's what you would describe as a slight variation?

There was another long pause. Miss Somers was being sucked deeper into the trap Mrs. Smith had prepared.

Her attorney rescued her. "Do you understand the question," he asked her.

A. No, I do not understand the question. . . .
ATTORNEY: The question was whether this is a slight variation.
A. There is a slight variation.

When we reviewed the hearing transcript and the results of our investigation, we knew that we had a very strong case. Unfortunately, the litigation might take years. However, we decided to sue Miss Somers, Standard, and Transworld Publishing not only for an injunction, but for mass restitution to deceived consumers.

When I'd met with Byers before submitting the Department's final amendments to the Consumer Protection Law, I had agreed to submit, at his request, one amendment that he said industry strongly favored and which did not appear to harm the consumer's interest. The Consumer Protection Law therefore provided that prior to instituting a mass restitution action, the Commissioner was required to send the prospective defendants a letter announcing her intentions, and giving the persons or companies five days in which to prove that they hadn't violated the law. I little suspected, when I drafted that provision to please Byers, that it might be employed as an enormously useful weapon in the Department's arsenal.

On an earlier occasion, receipt of such a letter by the chairman of the board of a large, publicly traded corporation had nearly given him heart failure. It had provoked in him the standard reaction—a telephone call to City Hall to get us off his back—within hours. Since the Mayor's aides were reluctant to tell a Commissioner not to do her job, they cooled the tempers of this large campaign contributor not by telling Miss Myerson to lay off, but by complaining gently about the crude form of the legalistically phrased notice. That wasn't how things were done. Such formality was jarring.

Therefore, on this occasion, when we were again dealing with a corporate giant, Commissioner Myerson advised us to ease the blow by telephoning Transworld Publishing's general counsel, to say that the letter was about to be sent.

I therefore called Kansas to inquire of the general counsel, Stuart Hall, the names of the corporate officers and attorneys who should receive copies of the letter.

"Oh," Hall told me, "there must be some mistake. Perhaps you have some quarrel with Standard, but Transworld Publishing isn't involved. Transworld is just the parent corporation. It has nothing to do with any violations by Standard."

"We have proof," I told him, "that Transworld is responsible, too."

"That's ridiculous," he said. "You can't hold Transworld responsible."

"I should think that is for the court to decide," I said. "My only problem at this point is to find out to whom the letters should be addressed."

He gave me a name.

"Is that person authorized to receive such a letter on behalf of Transworld?" I asked.

"No."

"I must have some officer of Transworld," I said.

"Please don't involve Transworld," he said. "Your dispute is only with the subsidiary."

After we went around in circles for about ten minutes, he gave me the name I wanted, and we hung up. But no more than three minutes after the call was over, my telephone rang, and Hall was back on the line.

"Mr. Schrag, have you sent that letter yet?"

"No," I told him.

"Well, I really wish you wouldn't send it," he said. The point seemed obvious.

"Why not?" I asked. "It's just a letter. We can't start suit for another five days."

"Look," Hall said, finally. "I'll tell you. Transworld owns several television stations whose licenses are up for renewal by the Federal Communications Commission. These renewal applications are being challenged, and under the FCC's rules, we must show them any letters Transworld receives which threaten litigation. So how about addressing your letters only to Standard?"

It was a new ball game.

"I'm sorry," I said. "We think that Transworld was at fault, and we must sue Transworld. I can think of only one way to avoid sending the letter."

"What's that?" he asked, hopefully.

"To settle this case almost immediately."

"I'll fly to New York tonight and be in your office at ten in the morning," he told me. "Will you hold the letters until then?"

I said that I would.

In the first round of bargaining, Hall declared the company's willingness to dump Hilda Somers immediately. I told him that I had no doubt that one way or another, he would clean up the New York operation, and that although we would insist on several provisions in a consent decree ensuring that future customers, if any, were told only truthful statements, our primary concern was that Transworld cancel contracts and make refunds to the eight thousand customers it had deceived who were currently paying for magazines.

He was opposed to any cancellations or refunds, but he quickly perceived that there would be no agreement without them. He pointed out that even if people had been deceived, they might wish to continue receiving the magazines, and the Department should therefore not insist on cancellations and refunds for all.

It appeared that the cost of refunds and cancellations for all customers—over a million dollars—exceeded the cost to the company of having the FCC find out about our threatened suit. Our object was to find a settlement that would cost the company one cent less than the letter would. I told him, therefore, that we would not insist on refunds to everyone, regardless of their desires, but at the very least we would insist that the company poll all of the subscribers by mail to determine their preferences.

This turned out to be the correct strategy. He said that he would have to discuss our demands with the company's officers in Kansas. When he returned to New York the following week, he said that the company was unwilling to make a mass mailing to customers, or to undertake large-scale refunds or cancellations.

"Then there appears to be no basis for any agreement," I said. "We'll send our letters this afternoon. It's been very pleasant meeting you."

"Can't we work something out?" he asked. "Suppose we don't do a mailing, but you issue a press release about the settlement, and say that anyone who writes in a letter of complaint will receive a cancellation and a refund?"

"Press releases aren't always picked up," I noted, "especially when they concern big corporations that advertise heavily in the newspapers to which the releases are sent. But

I can think of a way to guarantee that people would notice. Suppose Transworld placed five full-page advertisements four days apart in each of the three major New York newspapers, advising the public of the settlement with the Department, and telling people to write in if they want a refund and a cancellation? You could also produce a one-minute radio spot to be played frequently on New York stations over a two-week period."

That took him by surprise, and he had to return to Kansas for more consultation. To encourage him to settle, I gave him a copy of his franchisee's form of collection letter, which he hadn't seen. He was shocked, and realized the bad publicity that would accrue to Transworld if this letter were made public in connection with a description of Standard's selling techniques.

When he returned, we reached quick agreement on a consent judgment. Standard would be enjoined from engaging in the deceptive selling and collection techniques which we had discovered, and agreed to pay the Department three thousand dollars to reimburse its costs of investigation.[3] It agreed to send a letter to its eight thousand currently paying customers, informing them of the Department's charges and offering refunds to everyone who was deceived.[4] Standard had to enclose with each letter a postage-paid envelope, preaddressed to the Department. For our part, we agreed that our press release about the settlement would mention only Standard, not Transworld. Hall recognized that astute reporters might make the connection, and print a story not about an obscure magazine company, but about its huge corporate parent; he was willing to take the chance that no reporter would be that clever. None was.

Up to this point in our dealings with Transworld, we had been highly successful in obtaining a settlement very favorable to consumers—indeed, a settlement worth $750,000 if everyone responded to the mailing—without going near a court. But a consent judgment, like any other judgment, must be signed by a judge. The last step, then, was taking the judgment, signed by the President of Standard and its attorney, to the court for signature. I assumed that getting it signed would be an automatic process, since there would be no contest.

I brought it to the clerk at 9:30 in the morning, hoping for action early that day so that we could issue the press release we'd prepared. When I returned at 2:00 P.M., I discovered that nothing had been done; the clerks hadn't even read the papers. I inquired of a succession of clerks, until one finally told me that nothing could be done until another clerk's office sent up the file.

"But there is no file," I protested. "This is a consent judgment. Everything is right here."

"So it is," said a clerk. "Well, you'll have to see Mr. Weiss." He motioned to an elderly clerk who was wearing an American flag pin in his lapel. I explained to Weiss what I wanted.

"Do you work for Jack Greenberg?" he asked me out of the blue.

I was startled because Jack Greenberg is the Director of the NAACP Legal Defense Fund, whose employ I'd left a year earlier.

"No, I don't, but I once did."

"Tell me something; is the pay there very good?"

"Not particularly," I said.

"Then why did you work for the NAACP?" he asked.

I had no idea where this was going, but I wanted my judgment signed, so I continued the discussion. It is common knowledge that you are in trouble in the state court if you don't get along with the clerks, since they advise the judges what to sign and what not to sign; the volume of business is so great that the judges are forced to rely heavily on the clerks' advice, which can therefore often be determinative.

"I worked for them because I believed in what they are doing," I said.

"Oh, let's not get into that because I don't want to use profanity," he said. "A girl once came in here who worked for the NAACP Legal Defense Fund. I asked her to tell me if Jack Greenberg would give free representation to the Jewish Defense League. I've yet to get an answer."

I pointed to the judgment I wanted signed. Weiss read it through.

"This is improper," he said. "A judge shouldn't sign this."

"Why not?"

"You say in here in great detail what the company shouldn't do. It's not right to regulate a business like that, no matter what they did. You should just say that they shouldn't engage in fraud and leave it at that."

"But they've agreed to this specific regulation!"

"Besides," he said, "there's nothing wrong with these practices that you're prohibiting. These things are just salesmen's puffery."

"It's a consent judgment," I repeated. "They've agreed."

"These provisions on cancellations and refunds are improper, too," he said. "You shouldn't order them to cancel subscriptions, because magazine companies cancel them anyway, whenever a customer wants."

"How do you know?"

"I know all about this. A guy knocked on my door and sold some subscriptions. Then, when I wanted to cancel my subscription to *Fortune*, they let me out right away and sent me a refund."

"May I ask why you cancelled your subscription to *Fortune*?"

"They carried an article by Charles Silberman on race relations. Now an article like that doesn't belong in *Fortune*. If he wants to write such an article, let him publish it in *Ebony*."

"How about my judgment? They consented to it. It's signed by their lawyers. And you know, this is no pushover company. This is a subsidiary of Transworld Publishing. They knew what they were doing when they signed this."

"Tell me something," Weiss said, "how come a guy like you, who works for the NAACP, then turns around and sues an ultra-liberal corporation like Transworld Publishing? I don't get it."

"I just enforce the law impartially," I said.

"Well, you might be putting this company out of business," he said. "The magazine industry is pretty shaky, you know." He paused. "On the other hand, it *is* an ultra-liberal company. I'll submit your order to the judge. Come back in an hour."

The judgment was signed. When I left the Department, two thousand forms were being completed and filed by Standard's customers; they would be forwarded to Standard for the processing of refunds in accordance with the judgment.[5] Two weeks later, Transworld Publishing stopped all sales by Standard and all its franchisees.

From cases like Standard we learned that the bigger they are, the harder they fall. Although large corporations can gyp more people than small ones, they are also far more vulnerable to governmental pressure. We began to develop our synapse theory of consumer law enforcement.

No company can maintain itself alone, without vital connections to the outside world, synapses over which flow, for example, supplies, credit, advertising, essential services, and manpower. A court suit was a strike at the heart of a company's deceptive practice, usually a strike that was deflected by a judge. But by blocking vital synapses, the Department could starve a company into submission. Our attempt to deprive Kramer's of the benefits of its Yellow Pages advertising was an early attack on a corporate synapse.

The larger a company, the more synapses it needs to survive. A publicly traded company, for example, has underwriters and dealers or exchanges synapses that closely held corporations may not. A mail order house has an advertising synapse that a door-to-door sales network may not. Since a company creates its own synapses in response to its own definition of its needs, it can usually be crippled by an attack on any one of them. Companies adapt to their interconnections with the world, and become dependent on them. Deprivation of a credit source, an advertising medium, or a supplier of raw materials is likely to be a severe blow to the system.

We discovered that we could locate at least one vulnerable synapse of almost any company, and attack it without going to court. In the case of Transworld Publishing, that synapse was its already doubtful television license renewal. When we advanced toward that synapse, the company melted.

But we learned that this rule had an ironic exception. Companies below a certain size had almost no discernible synapses—they did not advertise, had no credit, owned or leased no real estate, had no licenses, and obtained personnel by word of mouth. Kramer's came close to this model—its only advertising was in the Yellow Pages. Such companies were far more likely to cheat customers, at least in gross ways, than medium-size companies or corporate giants, yet they were far less susceptible to our law enforcement activities.

As time went by, we discovered that New York City had a vast underworld of such mini-companies, many of them using illegal techniques to sell door-to-door in low-income neighborhoods. We investigated a substantial number of them; often they would evade our grasp. We found that white collar criminals with modest goals and limited connections to the outside world of commerce could make it in America.

Fortunately for the public, such men become greedy. They want to make more money, faster. They thrive on their own success. Their companies get bigger, settle in one location, expand, make connections—synapses. Then they can be caught.

NOTES

1. Having to falsify the name and true location of this corporation is a little ridiculous, since its size and high rank among major American corporations is an integral part of the story. I ask the reader to indulge me by assuming that the parent company is big and famous.

2. Her lawyer's theory opposing our subpoena was interesting. He claimed that the City Charter only gave us power to investigate fraud generally, not particular individuals' complaints, as here. But most companies we investigated, including Enchanting, claimed that we could only investigate particular complaints, not business practices generally.

3. This was a token payment, of course, which only partly reflected the manpower we'd expended.

4. The letters were to read as follows:

Dear Sir:

The New York City Department of Consumer Affairs contends that certain sales representatives of our independent franchise dealers have made deceptive statements in connection with the sale of magazine subscriptions, such as that "the magazines were free," "the subscriber would only have to pay for postage or handling" or that the purpose of the sales call was to take a survey of reading habits. Standard Magazine Service does not condone such practices and has arranged with the Department to guarantee that anyone who may have been misled into signing a subscription contract because of such deceptive statements is released from any further obligations. A person who requests cancellation will get [a pro-rata refund].

If you believe you were misled in signing your subscription contract and you wish to have it cancelled, will you please set forth the specific facts on the enclosed sheet of paper, sign it before a witness who is over twenty-one years of age and not related to you and return it in the enclosed envelope within twenty days of the date of this letter to the Department of Consumer Affairs.

Along with the letter, Standard would send the customer a form reading:

I wish to cancel my subscription contract because I was misled to sign it by the following deceptive statements made by the sales representative:

_____

_____

_____

[signature and witness]

5. A substantial proportion of the customers seemed unable to cope with the simple form we'd devised; they left out the short statement of how they were deceived, or neglected to have their signature witnessed. And 2% of the people who sent in the refund form included a monthly payment in the envelope.

7 · War: The Case of the Cut-Up Body

PEOPLE SOMETIMES ask me to describe the most outrageous case I ever saw of exploitation of consumers. A leading candidate is the case of Foolproof Protection, Inc., which sold burglar alarms door-to-door.

Virtually all the complaints about Foolproof came from low-income people residing in the slums of New York: Harlem, the South Bronx, the Lower East Side, Jamaica, Central Brooklyn. We heard the story again and again. A salesman had come to the customer's home; in many cases, he arrived within hours after the police had been notified that the person's house had been robbed.[1] The company sold a remarkable package, designed to appeal to the residents of high-crime areas of the city. A Foolproof alarm would be installed immediately, which would ring in the police station and in the house or apartment itself if the home were robbed. The customer had a one-month free trial period, and could also cancel at any time and have the alarm removed. The customer was taking little or no risk, because the salesman knew that the Foolproof company did not sue people who could not afford to keep up their payments, nor did it garnishee their wages.

The price was only about fourteen dollars a month for three years (about five-hundred dollars), during which time the customer "would not have to worry about service," because the company retained ownership of the alarm. At the end of the three years the customer could buy the alarm for fifty dollars. For $19.98 a month plus $50—a total of $769.28—the company promised to include an attachment that would call the fire department in case of fire.

Bruce Ratner went to work on the case and found that almost everything the company's salesmen said was a lie. The alarms did not ring in the police or fire stations. The customers could not cancel at any time, or even within a month; the fine-print documents they signed obligated them to pay for three years even if they decided they no longer wanted the alarms. And of all companies in New York City, Foolproof was the fifth most frequent user of the courts; only three banks and the telephone company sued more often, making Foolproof the most frequent plaintiff of all sellers of goods in New York.

Furthermore, the Fire Department's Division of Fire Prevention was shocked when Ratner asked them to inspect the $769.28 model installed in a consumer's home. Its report to Commissioner Myerson criticized the quality and reliability of the alarm and suggested that the price to consumers was more than ten times the cost to the company:

> While this system could conceivably cause an alarm to sound in case of fire, its reliability and integrity are definitely compromised by the use of unmarked, possibly inferior, and poorly installed components and wiring method. . . . All of the alarm components, switches, wire relay, siren, heat detectors, etc. are unlabelled or of unknown origin. The entire system has been assembled and installed in a very low grade, poor workmanship manner.
>
> This installation could by no means be acceptable by any known electrical code or standard and its reliability as a fire and burglar alarm is questionable.

Using standard price catalogue knowledge and labor time cost figures it is my opinion that the approximate cost of the material for this alarm system, including labor and installation, would be under $75.

It should be noted that my figure of $75 is a material/labor cost judgment only, to which would have to be added a reasonable sum for overhead and profit.

The $75 worth of parts to which the fire department referred included only a bell or siren, two dry cell batteries, a relay, a metal box which was placed on the customer's wall, one toggle switch for testing, an off/on switch, a few wires, pressure-sensitive switches fitted into the customer's windows and, in the case of the $769.28 model, heat detectors. If a window were opened, the switches would cause the alarm to sound; however, because the alarm was of the inferior "open-circuit" type, it would not sound upon the mere cutting of its wires. A burglar who smashed the glass in a window and then reached in to cut the wire before opening the window would not trigger the alarm.

By the time we learned the pattern of Foolproof's sales technique, we'd had enough experience with the courts to know that we were unlikely to obtain swift and effective justice by their invocation alone. Before deciding upon some other strategy, we determined to learn everything there was to know about Foolproof. We got one early break that significantly accelerated the detective work.

In 1968, the City Council had passed a law requiring home improvement contractors in New York City to be licensed by the Department of Consumer Affairs. Early in 1970, a Department inspector had visited Foolproof's premises and, finding that the company made improvements in homes and had no license, had issued to it a summons for doing business without a license. Had Foolproof fought the summons, a court might have held that the law did not apply to burglar alarm installations. Or Foolproof might have done as some other home improvement contractors do—pleaded guilty to a succession of such summonses, and passed along to its customers the costs of the small fines doled out by the Criminal Court for having an unlicensed business.

But Sam Stone, the fast-talking businessman who was Foolproof's President, chose otherwise. He'd been in trouble before—in 1955 he was indicted, along with the corporation with which he was then connected, in connection with the sale of food freezers. The charges against him were dropped when the corporation pleaded guilty. After that, he'd established a finance company, which developed a notorious reputation for dealing with dishonest merchants and using a variety of harsh sales tactics. When the going got rough, Stone had abandoned the finance company and started Foolproof, which also ran afoul of the law. In 1970, the New York State Attorney General had investigated Foolproof and had concluded that it engaged in a number of illegal practices. But Stone had talked the Attorney General's office into accepting an extremely weak consent decree, which barely interfered with his business methods. By 1970, when the Department inspector had come to call, Stone had learned this rule: the way to avoid trouble with the government is to make a deal. Stone figured that if the Department wanted him licensed, he might as well be licensed. The fees were low, and at that time the new Department's reputation as a law enforcement agency was only beginning to be molded. Foolproof had applied for a license.

We had not, at that time, commenced any investigation of Foolproof, and for some reason, no one bothered to check the complaint files when Foolproof's application for a license was filed. In the absence of any opposition, it was routinely granted.

Thus, when Ratner began his investigation, he discovered that the company was one of the Department's licensees, and, as such, had a greater duty to disclose information than did other companies. We did not have to resort to the usual subpoena-and-hearing route to learn about Foolproof.

Ratner called the company and told them that he would like to visit its premises with a Department accountant and inspect the books. The official he spoke to readily agreed. But when Ratner and the accountant arrived, the receptionist denied they had an appointment, said no officers were on the premises, and refused them entrance.

After the Department sent Foolproof a formal letter of demand to inspect the books, Stone requested a meeting, and he brought with him two attorneys. One was Richard Toole, the company's full-time secretary and General Counsel, who initiated its dozens of lawsuits against consumers every week. The other was Lister Young, a politically connected attorney whose son had been appointed to a significant post in city government by Mayor Lindsay. The message of his presence was not lost on us, but our reaction was simply to get more angry and to prepare, as part of our developing strategy, for the possibility of eventual political intervention.

At the meeting, Foolproof agreed that Ratner and an accountant would visit the company's offices and examine the records; we did not divulge the purposes of the inspection.

The investigation revealed that we were dealing with a much larger enterprise than appeared on the surface. Although the company's midtown headquarters were unpretentious, it had seven or eight field offices all over the city, from which fleets of door-to-door salesmen operated. Each of its offices served a particular area of the city; in some areas, where it was useful in making sales, Foolproof employed an all-black sales force. The company's salesmen had sold 16,000 alarms during its three years of operation; 42% of them to persons who earned less than $6,000 per year. It had batteries of employees employed to enforce collections from consumers slow to pay. The company's accounts receivable amounted to over four million dollars.

Its connections to the outside world were also impressive. Foolproof was a subsidiary—the only active subsidiary—of a holding company, Detective Systems, Inc., which was publicly traded over the counter and listed every day in the *New*

York Times. The officers of Foolproof were identical with those of Detective. The price of Detective stock had been rising steadily and was currently selling at around seven dollars per share. The company had also obtained over a million dollars in loans from several well-known New York banks. The loans were secured by the money due from consumers.

In addition, Detective, the parent, had a stunning asset. It had signed an agreement with a major New York department store, which I shall call Bramson's,[2] to operate a "leased department" in the store's various branches. A Bramson's customer who wanted a burglar alarm would be visited by a Foolproof salesman; he would buy a Foolproof alarm using his Bramson's charge card, and would never know that he was not dealing with a Bramson's employee. For the use of its good name, Bramson's would get a significant cut of the gross.

Ratner spent three days scrutinizing Foolproof's records —and three nights, too. During the day, Stone would sit by him and look constantly over his shoulder, or talk to him nervously about what an honest company he ran, how anxious he was to obey all the laws. Sam Stone, like Morton Glasser, sold from morning to night, and probably sold in his dreams as well. A middle-aged entrepreneur who was delighted with the small empire he'd built, Stone talked all the time. Each day, Ratner listened patiently as Stone told him, for example, that the burglar alarm industry in New York was a haven for fraud, and that other companies were in flagrant violation of the law.

But at night, Stone would get tired and head for his stately home on the north shore of Long Island, leaving Ratner to lock up the office. Then Ratner would start the day's work in earnest, examining the business records until midnight, then hurrying home for a little sleep before beating Stone into the office in the morning.

In this manner, Ratner sized up his adversary, and learned some valuable information. For example, Stone told Ratner that the price of the alarms was high because the customer was paying for more than the parts of the alarm and its installation; he was paying for three years of service. But by painstaking analysis of service records late one night, Ratner determined that the most frequent service Foolproof provided was replacing dead dry cells, and that only a quarter of the customers ever requested even that much service.

Ratner also wanted to obtain, if possible, the names and addresses of a substantial number of Foolproof's customers. Although we had a few dozen complainants, many with sad stories of deception combined with serious financial hardship, it would be difficult to present most of them to a court. For a majority, testifying would be a serious psychological and financial burden, and their memories of the precise events that had occurred years before were sufficiently imprecise that Foolproof would have demolished them on cross-examination. A much larger list of customers, from which witnesses could be selected, was a desirable piece of information to collect.

Foolproof kept these names and addresses, as well as other pertinent information, on three-by-five cards, as well as on punched computer cards. Ratner had heard Stone tell Foolproof's comptroller to give the Department full cooperation, and the comptroller arrived at work much earlier than Stone, so at 8:30 one morning, before Stone arrived, Ratner asked the comptroller to show him the three-by-five cards.

"Do you mind if I xerox these?" he asked. "The Department will pay the costs of duplication."

"No, go right ahead," the comptroller told him.

For twenty minutes, Ratner labored over the machine, wondering how many names and addresses he could copy before someone changed the rules. The comptroller kept turning around and looking at him, and every time he did so, Ratner figured the jig was up; the question was, would the comptroller insist not only that Ratner refrain from further copying, but that he surrender the already copied names. At last the comptroller stood up and walked over.

"Mr. Ratner," the comptroller said, "it just kills me to see a lawyer spending his time doing clerical work. Here, let me get one of the girls to do this copying for you, so you can do something more important." He had a secretary copy the entire stack for Ratner.

Ratner's investigation of Foolproof's records confirmed an important suspicion. The 1970 New York State Legislature had passed a law[3] providing that a person who signed a contract brought to him by a door-to-door salesman could cancel the obligation within three days by notifying the company of his intention to do so. The law also provided that the salesman must notify the consumer of his right to cancel by handing the customer a stiff, perforated card containing, in English and Spanish, a prescribed, simple text. The notice said that if the consumer wanted to cancel, all he had to do was tear off the bottom half of the card, sign it, and mail it; the bottom half, by law, was pre-addressed to the seller.

Violations of this law were punishable neither criminally nor civilly, but a consumer not properly notified of his right to cancel continued to bear such a right . . . until three days after the company provided him with the statutorily required stiff card. As far as Ratner could determine from the records, Foolproof had never printed or distributed the cards to its new customers, although it had made at least twelve hundred sales since the law became effective on September 1, 1970.

Finally, Ratner's very presence at Foolproof's offices produced one surprising by-product. Two of the company's salesmen, disgruntled because Foolproof had not been paying them at the rate promised, contacted him and supplied him with extensive information about how they had been trained to sell the company's products. For example, their sales managers had instructed them to say that Foolproof had a policy of not suing customers who were in default. The salesmen claimed to be shocked to learn that the policy was exactly the opposite.

When Ratner returned to the Department with an accurate profile of the company, we reviewed our strategic options:

(1) We could sue Foolproof under the Consumer Protection Law. This course of action would involve a minimum of several months delay while we drew up our court papers, and the court might deny our request for a preliminary injunction, especially since a decision before trial affecting sales practices might seriously affect the price of the company's nationally traded stock. After a year of grappling, we might get a trial, but our witnesses' memories, already fading, would be considerably worse, and our case would not be an easy one to win.

(2) We could institute a Departmental proceeding to revoke or suspend the company's license as a home improvement contractor. This course could be commenced immediately, but we had the usual problem with the barely articulate, extremely frightened potential witnesses. An experienced Departmental official estimated that we'd need to present several dozen consumer witnesses to sustain a decision against the company. Furthermore, this did not really avoid delay, since a series of three courts could review Departmental licensing determinations, and they customarily stayed suspensions or revocations for the year or more that review required. Even if a revocation were ultimately upheld, Foolproof could continue to collect its four million dollars from deceived ghetto consumers; it could even continue to sell without a license, subject to the unlikely petty annoyance of having to defend periodic misdemeanor charges for operating without a license, and pay occasional fines if found guilty.

(3) We could attack the company's commercial synapses by contacting the big institutions on whose credit and friendship Foolproof thrived. The company could not last two months if the banks refused to renew their thirty-day loans, and would be in serious trouble if Bramson's terminated the leased department. Unfortunately this course of direct action was unlikely to work. Those institutions had to be considered foe, not friend, at least for the present. Collapse of the company would prevent the banks from recovering their money. The banks' interests were intertwined with those of Fool-

proof. As for Bramson's, Foolproof provided the store with a substantial profit for very little work.

But this strategy of pressure deserved tabling for later consideration. For example, if Foolproof's fraud were sufficiently exposed publicly, the banks and Bramson's might begin to fear that the glare of publicity would reflect on them. Furthermore, although Foolproof was strong and secure at the moment, if it began to falter, its companion protectors might become vultures, each eager to consume what was left of the carcass before the others could react.

(4) We could take unprecedented unilateral action to strike the company a hard and possibly mortal blow, based upon a violation that was not its most serious, but one whose enforcement could be accomplished by direct action. The twelve hundred customers who had purchased alarms since September 1, 1970, still had the right to cancel, because Foolproof had never given them the perforated cards required by law. If we notified them of this right, a substantial number of them might exercise it, and each cancellation would reduce Foolproof's assets by up to $550 in accounts receivable and would instantly reduce the company's current cash income. Furthermore, the law specified that a company whose contract is cancelled must refund payments made by the consumer. For all its four million dollars in accounts receivable, Foolproof was cash-short, and refunds would be particularly damaging.

This strategy, too, had its shortcomings. First, if it killed the beast, the fraud would be terminated, but if Foolproof was able to withstand it, we would have on our hands only a wounded animal, more desperate than ever and probably more ready to engage in harsh collection techniques to survive. The tactic would probably have to be a prelude to other enforcement action. Second, there was a chance, although a very minor one, that we were wrong about the law. The statute applied to door-to-door sales, and said nothing about leases, but Foolproof cast its contract in the form of an installment lease with an option to purchase. No cases had yet arisen under the new law; Foolproof might argue that it need not make refunds because the statute did not apply. Third, we had no really hard evidence that Foolproof had consistently violated this law; we had only the absence of evidence that it had complied. Fourth, if Foolproof claimed that the cancellation law did not apply to it, or even if it conceded the law's application, it might sue the city for damages for inducing breach of contract. While we were likely to win such a suit, we could just imagine how the Corporation Counsel would react to *that*. (We even feared that the Corporation Counsel would insist that a damage action by Foolproof be settled, and that the Department refrain from further punitive action against the company.) Finally, we knew that Foolproof had political connections, and there was an outside chance that we would lose our jobs for engaging in direct rather than judicial action. However, we were persuaded that this company was so evil that it would be an honor to be canned for punishing it.

We decided on this last strategy.

Our assault was carefully prepared for many weeks. We took pains to keep our plans secret, lest Foolproof pre-empt our strike by making its own, less flashy notification to its consumers, or suing to enjoin our intended action (thus alerting the Corporation Counsel), or invoking political muscle. Only six persons in the Department, including Commissioner Myerson, knew about our plan.

Taking the names and addresses of the twelve hundred post–September customers from the copied three-by-five cards, we prepared a mass mailing, which we kept under lock and key. Each envelope to a customer contained:

(1) a covering letter signed by Commissioner Myerson, in English and Spanish, informing the customer of his right to cancel his burglar alarm contract;

(2) two stamped post-cards, one addressed to Foolproof, and one addressed to the Department (as a check), each containing a cancellation message,[4] followed by a mailing label on

which we had typed the consumer's name and address and which we had pasted on. Thus, to cancel, the consumer had only to drop the cards in the mail, as stated in the Commissioner's letter; he did not even have to sign his name;

(3) a copy of the card, to be retained by the consumer;

(4) a formal opinion of the General Counsel of the Department, and of the Consumer Advocate, that the law applied to Foolproof's agreements;

(5) in case Foolproof reacted by suing people who cancelled and stopped paying, a list of all of the OEO Legal Aid offices in the City; and, the kicker,

(6) to enable consumers to make a rational choice about cancellation, a copy of the opinion we'd received from the Fire Department, that the alarms were worth only $75, plus profit and overhead.

We also made several contingency plans, in anticipation of the company's possible reactions. For example, we thought it likely that the company would sue some or all of the people who cancelled, and we did not want the burden of testing the propriety of our action to fall on their shoulders. So we prepared to sue Foolproof the day it demanded payment from any customer who cancelled; we would claim that telling a person that he owed money when actually he'd cancelled his contract was a misrepresentation of consumer rights under the Consumer Protection Law. Thus we could immediately put the applicability of the cancellation law into issue with no problem of a dispute about the facts which would necessitate calling witnesses. Also, we prepared to obtain legal assistance immediately for anyone who cancelled and was sued, so that the first person into court claiming rights based upon our action would have good representation.

We also prepared to test the last missing piece of information, but to do so at the last possible minute, lest our intentions be discovered by Foolproof while there was time to preempt. After everything had been prepared, and the envelopes stamped, Ratner called Richard Toole, Foolproof's General

Counsel and collection lawyer, and engaged him in discourse concerning several minor aspects of the company's forms. Even at this point we were prepared to abandon the plan if there seemed any reason to do so. After about ten minutes of meandering conversation, Ratner asked offhandedly, "By the way, has Foolproof been giving out the three-day cancellation cards under last year's state law?"

Equally offhandedly, Toole replied, "Oh, no, that's one of the laws we haven't gotten around to complying with yet."

We mailed the letters early on a Friday morning, late in February, and that afternoon, as a matter of courtesy, Ratner went to see Stone to tell him what we had done. Although Stone said that he would receive him, the office was virtually empty when Ratner arrived; it seems likely that a leak to the company occurred that morning, as soon as the mailing was made known generally within the Department. Toole received Ratner, and heard the news grimly. "We're very bitter about this, you know," he said.

A few days later, I received a not entirely unanticipated telephone call from one of the Mayor's aides. He was apoplectic. "What gives you the right to notify a company's customers that they can cancel their contracts?" he screamed. "What law says you can do that? Where is it in the statute books? I want a brief on my desk by nine o'clock tomorrow showing me that you have that right. The Mayor works a twenty-hour day to keep businesses from moving out of New York and you scare them away! Did you research the Department's authority to do this? Who made the final decision to do this, anyway?"

"Commissioner Myerson," I happily told him.

That stopped him, but just for a moment. "Did you consult the Corporation Counsel?"

He ranted and raved for twenty minutes. At every chance he gave me to speak, I described to him (as whoever had spoken to him from the company had not) what the company did to its customers. Eventually he came to see that this might not be one of the companies that the Mayor worked day and night to keep in New York. Finally he calmed down, retracted his demand for a brief, and insisted only that he be notified before the Department again sent out such a mailing to a company's customers.

One aspect of our mailing which we thought clever turned out to be extremely important: we deliberately did not phrase our notice in the form prescribed by the statute—the form which starts the three-day cancellation period running. Therefore, consumers who received our mailing could cancel at any time, even after they were sued, months or years later, unless Foolproof meanwhile sent them a new notice in the proper statutory form. In the interim, the rights of consumers slow to respond would be preserved, and Foolproof's books would have to reflect the fact that all twelve hundred of its contracts since September 1, 1970 were in jeopardy.

The results of the mailing were gratifying. Over a three-week period, 376 customers cancelled, wiping out $190,000 of Foolproof's accounts receivable. Approximately 140 envelopes were returned to the Department because the addressee had moved without leaving a forwarding address. Of the remainder, 35% of the mailing's recipients cancelled. We kept a separate count of customers with Spanish surnames, and the same proportion (35%) of these customers cancelled. However, the majority of cancellation cards were mailed after the first three days following the mailing, suggesting that "cooling-off-period" laws, such as that of New York, which provide only three days to think over a transaction, may give buyers insufficient time to make a decision.

At about the same time, we decided to institute a license revocation proceeding against Foolproof, on the theory that even if final action in such a proceeding were months or years away, the Department ought to begin such a case. We served Foolproof with a complaint containing a wide variety of allegations. We alleged twenty-seven different instances of fraud or failure to perform by Foolproof, which we were prepared to prove by testimony of consumer witnesses, and listed eighteen other types of violation of the licensing law, such as the company's failure to keep the Department informed of the names of its salesmen or the location of its offices. One "count" in this complaint referred to a brochure we had obtained in which Foolproof stated that it "saves 55 lives per month."

The witnesses lived in every part of the city, but each one had to be interviewed before the hearing. Ratner sought the cooperation of the Legal Aid Society, and set up evening interviewing schedules in Legal Aid offices in every borough. Once again, the Department's lawyers worked days and nights. As they talked to the complainants, Ratner and his investigators became more and more angry, and more and more determined to insure not only that Foolproof cease its fraudulent practices, but that Sam Stone be stopped from repeating this pattern by using other corporations year after year.

Shortly before the hearing was scheduled to take place, Foolproof made its move. It informed the Department, through the reputable law firm of Downe, Sanders, and Hammerman, that it wanted to negotiate. The law firm explained to us, somewhat apologetically, that it did corporate and securities work for Detective Systems, Foolproof's holding company parent, and had been called specially into this case because of the serious consequences that license action might have for the parent as well as the subsidiary.

The demand for negotiation produced something of an internal crisis within the Department. As everywhere, militancy was exhibited in inverse proportion to seniority. The investigators, who had been interviewing the victims day and night, were altogether opposed to any compromise, and wanted simply to revoke the license. Ratner was mildly opposed to discussions with Foolproof. Fearing court delay during review of the license determination, I was mildly in favor of negotiating. The Commissioner settled it: a government agency had an obligation to hear out a party, even if it rejected compromise.

So we heard Foolproof's arguments for compromise, which were astounding. First, Foolproof contended that it was improper to punish the company for the acts of a few door-to-door salesmen. The company had instructed the salesmen to obey the law; Stone and the other corporate officers claimed not to have known about the "55 lives" brochure, for example, which had been written by one of the regional sales managers without authorization. We should perhaps reprimand the individual salesmen, but the corporation was not responsible. Second, if we did put Foolproof out of business, a vacuum would be created, and it would be filled by smaller, less reputable companies which would be impossible to control and would engage in even more vicious tactics. Finally, Foolproof's lawyers told us, in tones reminiscent of the Mayor's aide, to put this company out of business would adversely affect thousands of stockholders and would cause hundreds of employees, many of them black, to become unemployed. Even if the company were as bad as we said, were we prepared to cause such harm to innocent stockholders and employees?

"Do you mean," asked Henry Stern, our Deputy Commissioner, "that we can revoke the license of a little company that is cheating people, but that we should be more hesitant to revoke the license of a big company that is cheating even more people, because many employees would lose their jobs?"

"That's exactly what I mean," replied the man from Downe, Sanders, and Hammerman.

We decided that we had to negotiate, at least for a while. If hundreds of people were threatened with unemployment, and we refused even to talk, it might be difficult to convince City Hall of the propriety of our strategy. If, on the other hand, we talked, and Foolproof rejected our terms, no matter how harsh, City Hall was most unlikely to second-guess the details of our position.

However, we made up our minds that the settlement, if one were negotiated, would be the toughest in the history of consumer protection in the United States.

Stone and his lawyers negotiated with us for days at a time during nearly a month. Neither side mentioned its core interests or soft spots. Our undisclosed weak points were (1) our belief that if the negotiations collapsed, and we had to proceed with the licensing hearing, real changes, after all appeals, might be two years away, and (2) our fear that Foolproof would sue the city for $190,000 damages as a result of our mailing.

Their weak points, mentioned but never emphasized, were (1) their fear that publicity, particularly publicity mentioning Detective, would depress Detective's common stock, and (2) their fear that if the proceedings heated up sufficiently, Bramson's and the banks might turn against them.

We insisted, as a precondition to the negotiations, that while we were talking, Foolproof employees were not to resell, threaten, or even contact the 376 customers who had cancelled. These people, for whom we bore special responsibility because they had acted upon our information, were also among our major concerns in the bargaining that followed. Foolproof wanted to "renegotiate" their contracts by offering them as much as a 50% discount to sign up again. We eventually agreed on a freeze on such contracts during negotiations. Thereafter Foolproof could attempt a resale, by strictly truthful sales techniques, but only one man could go to make the pitch, and he had to hand a refund check to the customer who had cancelled before he could even begin the resale pitch.

Our next concern was with refunds or cancellations for the people to whom Foolproof had sold alarms in the past— the people who owed it four million dollars. We wanted Foolproof to mail them a questionnaire to determine whether they had been deceived, and to refund money to any customers who had been misled. Stone insisted that his customers would lie, and would say they had been misled just to get cash refunds. For days we circled this point, unable to reach any agreement. Finally, I told Stone that since we insisted on the point, we had better go ahead with the licensing proceeding, and with our other plan for getting refunds for the customers. I explained that nature of a mass restitution action. He quickly realized that not only were all of Foolproof's assets threatened for the first time, but that the pendency of such a suit would have to be disclosed in Detective's annual reports and future prospectuses to stockholders.

"Isn't there some way to determine without a mailing those few people who may have been misled?" Stone asked.

I explained an alternate plan. Foolproof would pay $25,000 to hire an impartial arbitrator for a year and equip him with an office. We would mutually agree on a procedure for selection of such a person, who, once hired, could not be fired. He would use any means at his disposal, within a year, to contact and personally interview Foolproof customers, and his word would be final as to whether or not they had been misled.

Stone took this plan seriously enough so that we began drafting a budget—$6,000 for office space, $700 for xerox, etc. He said he could live with the idea, provided that the costs did not exceed $25,000.

However, at the start of the next session, he said that he could not accept the open-ended risk of losing all his contracts, even if he could agree to the method for selection of the arbitrator. His customers, he was certain, would lie convincingly to the arbitrator. Would we accept any other terms?

Ratner and I exchanged glances. When we had drawn up our list of demands, we had drafted a provision so radical that we had not even presented it to Stone. This seemed to be the time to take it off the shelf and dust it off. "Mr. Stone," I said, "you claim to want to run an honest business, but your record is very bad. Your salesmen seem incapable of making an honest presentation to a low-income consumer, and we view with alarm the fact that the ghetto is your major market. Consumers who are less educated are more easily taken in, and it is just these consumers who can least afford to be cheated. We will abandon our demand for a survey of your past customers if you agree to get out of the ghetto."

To our surprise, Stone readily agreed.

"No more sales to any customers having weekly salaries below $155 a week," Ratner said. "And to police compliance, you will have to have your customers fill out credit applications open to our inspection, stating their salaries, and you cannot accept a contract unless the customer's employer verifies that he earns more than $155."

Stone insisted on two modifications, which we agreed to: first, the critical salary figure was to start at $100, and to rise to $155 on a sliding scale over a period of nine months, and second, the limitations would not apply to Bramson's customers who had held Bramson's charge accounts for ninety days before buying an alarm.

Our next demand was that Foolproof employ a series of devices to ensure that no customer with a legitimate grievance would be sued. All dunning letters would have to encourage recipients to notify the company of any complaints on the self-addressed, stamped reply postcards included with the letters. A final dun had to hint at possible misrepresentations by saying, "We hope you are satisfied with your burglar alarm, which alerts you to intruders and, as you know does not ring at the police station. We told you before installation that installation was not free, that there was no trial period, and that your agreement could not be cancelled for three years. If you have any complaints regarding sales, service or the above facts, please mail us the enclosed card so that we can make whatever adjustment is appropriate." The pre-stamped card enclosed with this dun was to be addressed to Foolproof at the Department's post office box; the Department would monitor the mail.

Foolproof would have to respond to each such complaint by putting the consumer in the position he would have been in if the salesman had been telling the truth. For example, if the customer had been told that the alarm would ring in the police station, Foolproof would have to provide him with that type of alarm (sold commercially for approximately $1,000).

If the company received no response and sued, it would

have to attach to its summons a list of names and addresses of all the Legal Aid and OEO Legal Services offices in the city.

After several negotiating sessions, Stone accepted these restrictions.

Next, to ensure fair dealing in the future, we insisted that salesmen be made to say the opposite of all of their former misrepresentations. They would henceforth have a duty to disclose, orally and in writing, that the alarms they were selling were *not* connected to the police station, that Foolproof sues people who do not pay, and so forth. Furthermore, before installing an alarm, Foolproof would have to send each new customer a letter asking whether the salesman had made each of the required affirmative disclosures, and give the customer a stamped card for reply. No contract would be valid if the customer reported that any disclosure had been omitted.

Stone readily accepted this demand also. "What the salesman says won't hurt the sales," he confided candidly. "You want me to say that the alarm isn't connected to the police station, I'll have the men say, 'You know, this alarm will ring in your home, to frighten off the burglar, without causing unnecessary disruption by signaling the police.'"

We had a number of less innovative demands as well: that Foolproof immediately settle the individual complaints that had been filed with the Department, that Foolproof stipulate that any claims it might have against the city for the mailing to customers were settled (we raised this incidentally, although it concerned us throughout the negotiations), that Foolproof accept a reprimand and fine on its licensing record, and that the company pay the Department costs of $2,500. We also insisted that within twenty days after the out-of-court settlement agreement was signed, Foolproof and Stone sign another document consenting to a court judgment embodying, word-for-word, the terms of the earlier agreement, so that Stone would be liable for a jail sentence for contempt if he violated his promise.

Agreement neared. Stone and his battery of lawyers had accepted virtually every one of our demands. There remained the issue of publicity, which Stone had wanted to discuss at the outset. At that time, however, I'd told him that I was not authorized to discuss publicity, because I was merely the prosecutor. He would have to take up that matter with Henry Stern. This tactic enabled us to avoid early compromise of the publicity issue; it made it impossible for us to trade off publicity for additional enforcement provisions.

Stone brought his Vice-President, Hugh Wood, as well as his lawyers, to the meeting with Stern. They requested the right to edit any press release that the Department planned to issue before they signed the agreement. Stern flatly refused to permit "negotiation" of a press release, and added that he expected that in any event, no press release would be issued until at least twenty days later, when the subsequent judgment was entered. Stern wanted to ensure that this document was signed before the publicity cooled our relationship. They then made two demands to which the Department agreed: that the release mention only Foolproof, not the publicly traded parent, Detective; and that it not mention Bramson's. A meeting was scheduled for the afternoon of Friday, March 26, to sign the settlement.

The day before the document was to be signed, we began to get telephone calls from Foolproof customers who had cancelled. Salesmen had come to their homes and frightened them into agreeing to remain as customers. One consumer complained that the Foolproof salesman had kept his hand in his trenchcoat pocket, and he feared that he had a gun.

Nearly everyone who called had already been visited by a Foolproof salesman; some had re-signed, and some had not. Foolproof was breaching the agreement before it was even signed; these visits were a violation of our interim understanding that there would be a moratorium on visits, as well as a violation of the provisions of the agreement governing conduct during any resale negotiations.

One woman had not been visited; the Foolproof salesman said he would come to her house that evening, Thursday,

March 25. Enraged, Ratner rushed to the woman's home and planted a tape recorder.

The next day, when Stone and his lawyers arrived to sign the agreement, I protested about the visits. Stone admitted that visits had been made, and claimed not to recall the interim understanding, which had not been written down. I asked him whether the visits had been conducted in accordance with the provisions of the agreement about to be signed, and he assured me that they had. "Has each salesman handed over a refund check before commencing his pitch?"

"Surely."

"Has he made the affirmative disclosure required for all sales?"

"Yes."

"Have the salesmen, in commenting on the cancellation letters sent by the Department, disparaged the Commissioner, or the Department or its employees?"

"Don't be ridiculous," said Stone. "They haven't even mentioned the Department to customers."

"I'm glad to hear it," I said.

Stone read and initialed each page; then he and the lawyer from Downe, Sanders signed. I gave them copies and filed the original away before commencing Act Two.

Then I produced a small tape recorder and placed it on my desk. An apprehensive look crossed Stone's face. "Now, Mr. Stone, I am going to do you a favor. All along, you have complained that you were innocent because you had no idea what your salesmen were doing, and you couldn't control them. But as our negotiations progressed, you said that you would be a model citizen, and would exercise the strictest control over the tactics employed in the name of your company. Then, a few minutes ago, you assured me that your salesmen who visited customers who cancelled did not disparage the Department or violate the terms we had agreed upon for the procedure for such visits. I am now going to demonstrate to you that even on the eve of signing this agreement, you were not in control of your company, and you did not know what your employees were doing." I turned on the recorder, and played for Stone and his lawyer the recording Ratner had made in Brooklyn the previous night.

"Good evening," said the salesman. "As you know, I'm here to explain about that letter you received from the Department of Consumer Affairs. You know, Bess Myerson wants to make a big name for herself, so she can run for public office. And Foolproof is a big company, so its books are open for inspection any time by the government. So Bess Myerson sent some young punk up to our office to look over our books, and while he was there this fellow noticed that a few of our contracts were missing a clause required by a new law. We had made up new contracts, but we accidentally used a few of the old ones, and yours was one of them. So this punk, wanting to get a pat on the back from some big supervisor,[5] told Miss Myerson to send out those letters.

"Now you can cancel if you want to, but I'd just like to know why you want to cancel, and find out if we did anything wrong."

"Well, the salesman who came here told me the alarm would make a loud noise, so that it could be heard all over the neighborhood," said the woman. "But one day, my husband came in from work and accidentally set off the alarm and he didn't know how to turn it off. It rang for hours in the apartment, but nobody could hear it in the street. When I came home from work later, I didn't even know it was on until I actually entered our apartment. I don't think it would work, because no one but the burglar could hear it."

"But that's not the company's fault," the salesman explained, "that's because you have an old building. If you lived in a newer building, it could be heard on the street.

"Anyway," he continued, "half the purpose is alerting you if you are asleep during a burglary. Alerting neighbors to a break-in while you are away from home is important, but the most important purpose of a burglar alarm is to wake you up if there is a burglar in the house, and frighten him off.

After all,"—the salesman's words became slower, measured, —"a stereo, a hi-fi, a suit of clothes can always be replaced. . . ." His voice fell to a near-whisper, "but God forbid, a cut-up body will always bear a scar, or, God forbid, require an amputation."

The salesman let that sink in, and then continued his pitch. The company, he told the woman, would be willing to make a reasonable deal. First, he offered her a discount to $90 if she would recommit herself to retaining the alarm. When she refused this offer, he raised the discount to $120, then $240, then $360, and finally $400. She consistently refused him, and finally he left the house. At no time did the salesman hand her a refund check or make the disclosures required by our understanding with Stone.

Stone and his lawyer sat mute for ten seconds after I turned off the recorder. Then Stone picked up my telephone, dialed his office, and told his sales manager, "Stop all re-selling immediately. I want to see all the salesmen in the central office first thing Monday morning." I began to think that the company might be capable of reform.

I was soon disillusioned. During the next few days, people who had cancelled continued to call, reporting new visits by Foolproof salesmen which did not comply with the terms of the agreement. Three times within two weeks, we summoned Stone to the Department to explain what appeared to be violations of the settlement. Each time he said that he'd misunderstood the meaning of the settlement, and each time we permitted him to sign a new stipulation, clarifying the settlement and strengthening the enforcement provisions, instead of suing him. One such stipulation, for example, required him to notify Ratner in advance when appointments were made to visit customers who had cancelled, so that the Department could randomly select 10% of such visits to plant concealed records. Stone said he had no objection to such recording, because he would tell his salesmen that we were secretly recording *all* of their visits.

On April 14, 1971, when Stone and his attorney came to

sign the consent to the entry of judgment, he requested that entry of judgment and its attendant publicity be deferred for ten more days, to which I agreed.

Word of our mass cancellation and settlement began to spread to other agencies, and some of them, including the Federal Trade Commission, the United States Attorney and the Bronx District Attorney, began or intensified their own investigations of Foolproof. The Attorney General of New Jersey, who had been working on the case for several months, sued Foolproof for fraudulent practices in the sale of its alarms there. On the first day of the suit, a court signed a temporary restraining order enjoining Foolproof from collecting any money on any outstanding contracts in New Jersey, or on any *judgments* it had obtained in the New Jersey courts. We were amazed by the order, because the New Jersey courts seemed so much more prepared to deal swiftly with consumer fraud than their New York counterparts. Stone was even more amazed, because the order immediately cut off 5% of his revenue. Coming only a few weeks after our mailing, it was a serious financial blow to the company.

Also, Stone had disclosed to Bramson's that he'd had some trouble with the Department, but told the store that it was now settled. Bramson's lawyer came to see me, to ask what had happened. I gave him a copy of the settlement, without making any recommendation that Bramson's take any action against Detective. I did ask that he give me a copy of the contract between Bramson's and Detective, and he refused. This attitude confirmed my earlier suspicion that it would not have been productive, at the outset, to ask Bramson's not to deal with a company merely because it was cheating its customers.

On April 27, I took the papers that Stone had signed to the clerk's office of the State Supreme Court for signature by the judge. Mr. Weiss greeted me from behind the desk and took the papers. He read through the decree, very slowly.

"This is improper," he said. "I'm going to recommend to the judge that he not sign it."

"Why not?" I asked.

"This decree goes into too much detail, regulating every aspect of this company's business."

"But that's necessary for enforcement," I argued. "They signed a consent decree once before, with the Attorney General, but it didn't do the job. We've got to make it specific to make it work."

He shook his head. "Besides, it's too long, six pages single spaced. Judgments shouldn't be so long. The judge shouldn't have to read so many pages. And neither should I. It's an imposition. It's not my job."

"Is that all that is wrong with it?" I asked.

"No, that's not all. You have a long section in here regulating their collection procedures. That's improper. When someone owes his creditor money, the creditor should be able to collect any way he wants to short of violence. This company sells to a lot of Negroes, doesn't it?"

"Yes."

"Well, you know as well as I do that Negroes don't pay their debts on time."

"Many of these people have been defrauded," I told him. "They need special protection so that they can defend themselves."

"Then let them come into court and defend themselves," he said.

"Look," I said, getting worried, "this is nothing new. Attorney General Lefkowitz has been getting consent decrees regulating selling and collection practices for years."

"Lefkowitz is making it impossible for a man to run a business in this state," Weiss replied. "And Lindsay is making it impossible to run a business in the city. Lindsay is without a doubt the worst Mayor New York ever had," he told me. "He even makes Wagner look good."

"Are you in politics?" I asked.

"I was a Conservative Party candidate for election as a judge of this court in the last election," he said, "but I lost."

"Well, will you present these papers to the judge?" I asked.

"No, I told you I thought they were improper," he said. "But I will present them to the Chief Clerk, with the recommendation that he recommend to the judge that they not be signed. Come back in two hours."

When I returned, Mr. Weiss told me that the chief clerk had decided, against his better judgment, to submit the papers to the judge without any recommendation. An hour later, to my great relief, the judgment was signed.

That afternoon, the Department issued a strong press release which began: "A burglar alarm company that sold its alarms for seven times their cost by falsely stating that some were connected to police stations has consented to a court judgment halting its unfair sales practices." The release mentioned the mailing we had undertaken, but, in accordance with the Department's assurances, did not state the name of the company's parent corporation. The *New York Times* described the judgment on the first page of its second section the next day; other newspapers gave the story minor coverage, or none at all.[6] Publicity did not affect the price of Detective stock, which hovered around seven dollars per share.

Almost immediately, Foolproof began violating the judgment. Complaints began to come in from new customers of the company as well as from those who had cancelled their contracts. In some cases, consumers called between the time a salesman made an appointment for a home visit and the time he was scheduled to arrive; we were able to send an investigator with a tape recorder. In one case, we recorded a salesman making a presentation that violated virtually every obligation the company had under the judgment; we called the salesman in for a hearing, and he not only conceded the violations under oath but admitted that the presentation he made to that consumer was typical of several others he had recently made.

We also began receiving complaints from burglar alarm customers of Bramson's, and we decided to do our own investigation of the department store as well. Several investigators posed as customers and asked Bramson's to send a burglar alarm salesman to their homes. They recorded the presentations, and we found that even when selling under Bramson's name, Foolproof salesmen were unable to restrain themselves from exaggeration.

During this period, we sent Stone a steady stream of individual complaints to resolve. Although we pressed him regularly, he did not resolve them promptly. His failure to pay prompt attention to the individual consumers who said they had been gypped, together with the developing evidence of continuing violations, caused us to summon him to yet another meeting, at which we showed him the transcript of the hearing at which his salesman, accompanied by Foolproof's General Counsel Richard Toole, had admitted a number of violations. We threatened enforcement action unless Stone agreed to pay a new fine and to sign a new stipulation promising prompt refunds to individuals who complained of deception. Stone said that he would have to think it over; a few days later, he refused.

We then heard from a new law firm—his fourth group of attorneys during our brief relationship—that all our future contact with the company should be through them. My first contact with this firm was a request that it supply me with copies of the Foolproof credit applications which we were entitled to inspect under the provisions of the agreement and judgment. The attorney I spoke to promised to call me back with a response in three days. He never called back. Having lived through the Enchanting Wigs case, I was not prepared to beg repeatedly for documents that the Department had a right to inspect.

These developments completely altered our relationship. For two months, the company and the Department had been circling each other, feeling out areas of mutual agreement; the Department had used each new piece of evidence to tighten the screw, but ever so slightly, and Stone was becoming a familiar figure in the Department's offices. Now we were dealing at more than arm's length, and it was total war.

A direct action rather than a judicial approach had worked so far, and we continued to apply that strategy. The company's armor was disintegrating under the blows it had received: the contract cancellations, the restrictions it had agreed to, the New Jersey suit, and the *New York Times* publicity. Now its synapses were exposed. I informed the General Counsel of Bramson's that we had evidence that the store had been violating the city's Consumer Protection Law, and requested that Bramson's voluntarily supply the Department with various documents concerning its sales of alarms, including its contract with Foolproof. It was implicit that if voluntary cooperation was not forthcoming, I would issue a subpoena.

Bramson's sent one of its attorneys to see me. "We hate like the devil to be investigated," he told me. "We didn't know anything about Detective's tactics until we heard about them from the Department. We'd had a few complaints, but they just seemed to indicate that there were some overly zealous salesmen. We were impressed by the fact that we were dealing with a publicly traded company. We felt that offered us protection."

I told him that we had not reached any firm conclusions about Bramson's culpability, that we were still investigating, which is why we wanted the documents.

"If we terminate our contract with Foolproof," he asked, "will you still insist on investigating us?"

"If you're not selling any burglar alarms," I said, "I don't see how we could fruitfully devote our resources to investigating your sale of burglar alarms."

Bramson's terminated its agreement with Detective the next week.

Even before that termination, Detective's stock had started to slip. The slide began weeks after the publicity hit, but once it started, it continued steadily. Seven—six—five—four—three. After Bramson's terminated, the stock hit a low of seven eighths of a dollar.

And then a new development occurred which drastically altered the character of the case. A man called to complain that he had bought Detective stock at seven dollars, on the recommendation of Optimum Analysis Corporation, a public relations firm. The firm had never mentioned that the company was in trouble, and immediately after his purchase, the price of the stock had declined dramatically. He offered to send us a copy of Optimum's report on the stock, and we urged him to do so.

The report was astonishing. Although it was dated "March 1971" and purported to be based upon information received from Sam Stone, the company's President, it contained no mention of the $190,000 loss caused by the consumer response to the Department's late February mailing, of the agreement signed late in March, or of the New Jersey Attorney General's suit initiated late that month. Ratner went to see Victor Berlin, President of Optimum.

Berlin clasped and unclasped his hands throughout the interview. "I was waiting for you fellows to show up here," he said. "Several times I almost called you myself. I've been living with this thing for over a month now. My reputation is ruined. What will I do?"

Ratner urged him to start at the beginning.

Berlin, it developed, had first heard of Detective in February 1971, when he had received a letter from one of its attorneys, on the stationary of Downe, Sanders, and Hammerman, requesting that Optimum issue a report on the company in the near future. Berlin had agreed, in large measure because the request had come from a prestigious law firm. Throughout February and March he met with Stone and the Vice-President, Hugh Wood, and had received highly favorable information indicating that the company would do well. On the basis of the information, Berlin had written a glowing report, which Stone signed, and had mailed it to over a hundred stockbrokers in the New York area. Stone and Wood had never mentioned that they were simultaneously in negotiations with Ratner and myself, nor had they said anything about the 376 consumers who had cancelled their contracts.

A few weeks later, Berlin read in the newspapers that the company had suffered unusual losses and had consented to a far-reaching judgment. As the price of the stock fell, Optimum's clients became angry, and accused Optimum of misleading them. Berlin's credibility had been destroyed, and his attorneys were preparing a damage action against Detective and Stone.

Meanwhile, impressed by the information they had received, Berlin and several other employees of Optimum had themselves bought large quantities of Detective stock at seven dollars a share. When the bottom dropped out, they themselves had lost substantial sums.

"Incidentally," Berlin said, "watch that fellow Hugh Wood. He used to be at Endowment National Bank, when the bank gave Detective a million dollars in loans. After that deal was completed, he left Endowment to become a Vice-President and Director of Detective and Foolproof. You watch him."

We watched him. We consulted the Securities and Exchange Commission's official summary of stock transactions by corporate "insiders"—officers and directors. Wood had attended two of the sessions at which Stone and his lawyer had negotiated the agreement with the Department of Consumer Affairs. That agreement was signed late in the afternoon on Friday, March 26, 1971. The following Monday, weeks before the agreement was publicized, Wood had sold 1,200 shares of Detective. It was not inconceivable that the company's insiders had used Optimum to keep the price of the stock steady for a short period while crucial sales were made. Commissioner Myerson advised the SEC to investigate.

The stock continued to fall. By consulting records at the SEC, we learned that while Stone claimed not to own any publicly traded shares of Detective, and disclaimed beneficial ownership of his wife's shares, he did own over half a million dollars worth (at seven dollars) of restricted shares, which could not be sold on the market until the middle of 1972. The value of these shares was wiped out. Berlin called us with a new discovery: the previous owners of some of the shares he had bought while promoting the stock were partners in the law firm of Downe, Sanders, and Hammerman; they too had been selling.

Meanwhile, Foolproof was still selling alarms, and was still collecting on old contracts, and Richard Toole was still suing consumers at a furious rate, except in New Jersey, where the order obtained by the Attorney General put us to shame. We had to act.

We drew up a new license revocation summons—this time, one which would not require the presence or testimony of many consumer witnesses. We made two kinds of allegations: first, that the officers of the company were not of good moral character (a statutory standard for home improvement contractors in New York City) because they had violated the standards of conduct established by the federal securities laws, and second, that the company had violated the agreement with the Department. We served the company with papers, calling for it to appear on Monday morning, June 28, 1971.

I suspected the Foolproof's new lawyers would make some move to block the hearing, and I did not want to inconvenience the Department's witnesses by having them appear unnecessarily, so the previous week I called Spencer Cates, who was now handling the case for Foolproof. He conceded that he was preparing an application for a court order, but fearing my opposition, refused to reveal in which county he would apply.[7]

On Friday morning I called the motions clerk in each county and requested that I be telephoned and called to the court if Spencer Cates showed up trying to enjoin the Department of Consumer Affairs.

"What's the name of the company?" said the clerk in Queens.

"Foolproof Protection, Inc.," I said.

"Oh, sure we'll call you," he said. "Everyone knows they're a bunch of crooks. I've been reading about them in the newspapers."

Another clerk told me, "We won't call you, but we'll take this telephone call into account in deciding whether to issue the stay."

A third clerk, in Brooklyn, said he might call.

The fourth clerk, in Manhattan, told me: "Manhattan never stays a public agency."

By Friday night, I had heard nothing from either Cates or the clerks. I concluded that we would have a hearing on Monday morning, and advised the witnesses to appear.

At ten in the morning that Monday, the witnesses had arrived, the hearing officer was seated at his desk, the prosecution was ready. But neither Cates nor anyone from Foolproof had appeared. Nor had we been served with any court papers. By 10:20, I knew something was wrong. I called Cates, who wasn't in; his secretary said that he had gone directly from his home to work on the Foolproof case. That could have meant that he was on his way to the hearing . . . or it could have meant trouble.

At 10:45, the hearing officer and the witnesses were getting restless. We could have started without Foolproof, since the company had defaulted—that would have been pleasantly ironic, since it had obtained thousands of judgments by default against consumers—but we thought it better first to establish definitely whether they were absent on principle or had merely been delayed in traffic. We opened the hearing for the record, and then, before we put on any witnesses, I called Cates' secretary again.

"Mr. Cates hasn't arrived at the Department yet," I said. "Do you have any idea where he might be?"

"All I know is he had some papers he went out to get signed."

"Can you tell me what county he headed for?"

"I think he said something about Queens."

That was all I needed to know. I called the motions clerk

in Queens. The man who answered was not the clerk who had read about Foolproof in the papers.

"Could you please call me if a Mr. Cates, representing Foolproof Protection, Inc., shows up in your court seeking to stay a hearing by the Department of Consumer Affairs?"

"Why, he's here at the desk in front of me right now!" said the clerk.

"Could I come right out to oppose his application?" I asked.

"How soon could you get here?"

"Twenty minutes."

"O.K., we'll wait twenty minutes," he said.

Ratner and I raced out to Queens. Cates was standing at the clerk's counter. I asked him for a copy of his application papers.

"Do I have to give him a copy?" he asked the clerk. "This is the part of the Motions Office for motions without notice. Schrag got notice accidentally, but he wasn't entitled to notice."

"Better give him a copy," the clerk said. "The judge might want to hear his side of it, too."

We leafed quickly through more than one hundred pages of affidavits and exhibits that Cates was presenting to the court. This was the move we'd been waiting for—Foolproof and Detective were staking everything on this motion, and throwing in all the ammunition they had. This was not merely an application for a stay of the hearing, but an application to hold a hearing on nullifying the consent judgment, so that we would both start off again at day one. The only ground for such an unusual demand is that the consent to the judgment was obtained by fraud and duress . . . and that is just what Foolproof claimed. In his affidavit, Stone gave his version of all that transpired, and described the negotiations as he had perceived them. He told the court, for example, of the plan for Foolproof to hire an impartial arbitrator, which Stone ultimately rejected. "Thereafter," Stone wrote, "Mr. Schrag, all of a sudden and completely out of character, became reasonable and suggested he would forget about the 'ombudsman theory' if we agreed to phase out of ghetto sales. . . ." However, "Mr. Schrag sét up onerous requirements in our reselling of cancelled customers. They attempted to prevent the salesman from doing any selling and make him a robot.

"The assurance of discontinuance," Stone continued, "was signed most reluctantly with the licensing proceeding pending and the Sword of Damocles hanging over Foolproof's head, well knowing that if it was not settled that the chances of keeping Bramson's were nil. . . . Simultaneously with our signing an assurance of discontinuance, Mr. Schrag placed a tape recorder on our desk and played a tape of one of our salesmen, who was unknowingly taped while trying to re-negotiate a cancelled sale. He had accused the Department of being unfair and politically motivated, which in my opinion is true, and he also dramatically reminded the customer of the risk of not having the burglar alarm, to wit, loss of property and risk of life. . . .

"I now realize that in signing the assurance of discontinuance I was not unlike Neville Chamberlain meeting with Adolf Hitler at Munich—I gave an inch and they took a mile."

"This way please," called the clerk, ushering us into the judge's chambers.

The judge leafed through the hundred pages for two or three minutes. Then he turned to me. "What harm would come if the Department's hearing were adjourned for a few days, until we can sort all this out?" he asked.

I was very unhappy about the prospect of even a short stay because of what I believe to be Newton's law of judicial inertia: a hearing, suit, or injunction in motion tends to remain in motion, but a proceeding that is stayed tends to remain stayed. I explained that the company was alleged to be gypping low-income customers all the time, that half a dozen government agencies were after it, and that the proper procedure would be to let the hearing continue, subject to Foolproof's right to apply for a stay if the Commissioner ruled against the company and the company appealed the ruling.

The judge then turned to Cates. "I think you've made this motion in the wrong county," he said. "You're trying to open a Manhattan judgment in Queens."

"But the statute . . ." said Cates.

"You should be doing this in Manhattan."

"I have no objection to applying in Manhattan," said Cates.

The judge turned back to me. "Will you consent to staying the hearing for two days so that he can go to the proper county with this motion?"

"I'm afraid I can't consent to that, your honor. In the next two days, this company will sell alarms to dozens of consumers. . . ."

The judge looked at me with shock. Evidently no lawyer had ever refused to consent to a delay he'd suggested. "If you don't consent, I'll *order* you to postpone the hearing," he roared. He still hadn't read the papers.

I consented.

I telephoned the Department to send the witnesses home. Then, in separate cars, Cates and we drove back over the bridge, to the motion clerk's office in Manhattan. The clerk looked over the papers and took us all in an elevator to the judge's chambers. On the way, he said he doubted that Cates was proceeding in the proper way; he thought Cates should apply for a stay after the hearing rather than before. This, together with my information that "Manhattan never stays a public agency," was very encouraging.

We stood together outside the chambers while the clerk went in and briefed the judge on the case. After about five minutes we went in. This second judge, hearing motions "without notice" that week in Manhattan, was an elderly, retired judge filling in. He hadn't had time to read the papers either.

"What's this case all about?" the judge asked Cates.

Cates explained that he was trying to re-open a judgment

obtained by fraud and duress by the Department, and to stay a Departmental hearing until his motion to reopen had been decided. (If he won the motion and reopened the judgment, half the grounds for the license hearing would disappear.)

"What harm will come if you hold off for a couple of days while I refer this to the judge who hears cases 'with notice'?" the judge asked me.

I tried again, but I couldn't persuade the judge that there was any urgency. He asked me to consent, again, to a two-day postponement of the hearing. I did.

We drew up very brief reply papers, and went to court, before a third judge, that Wednesday morning. This judge was vigorous, tough-minded, serious, and legally oriented. The argument lasted fifteen or twenty minutes, and centered around the stay, since the judge made it clear that he would not rule on the motion to vacate the judgment until he'd read the papers. After he heard where things stood, he dissolved the stay. Cates was furious. He kept protesting, pressing his argument. Although he'd made his decision, the judge heard Cates out, then reaffirmed that the stay had been dissolved.

Cates stormed out of the courtroom. In the corridor, I told him that the hearing would resume Friday morning. "Come hell or high water, we won't be there," he said. We confirmed the date to him by telegram.

True to his word, Cates did not show up on Friday. We presented the first half of our witnesses, who testified about the company's stock manipulations. The hearing was then adjourned until the following week.

Late that afternoon, the judge decided the case, refusing to reopen the judgment that Stone had consented to.[8]

Now Stone was in very serious trouble. He had staked everything on this legal maneuver, and he had lost. Bramson's had deserted him, several government agencies were proceeding against him, and the banks from which he borrowed were considering not renewing their loans. If they did not renew, Detective would probably fold; it did not have enough cash to repay.

The type of loan that Detective had obtained was called a "Chinese take-out" loan. Several banks participated. Endowment National, which had first made the loan, lent only for thirty days. At the end of that time, other, smaller banks, "took" Endowment "out" by paying the money to Endowment and accepting the risk that Detective would not pay, along with the interest for that month. Then, after another month, Endowment would again take over the indebtedness.[9]

Now it was Endowment's turn to take over the loan. It refused, leaving the smaller banks stuck with extending the term of the loan themselves, or calling the loan. But if they called the loan, Detective was likely to go bankrupt, and they would lose all chance of collecting. The banks would then have only the consumer contracts which secured the loan— and would face a difficult battle with the Department if they tried to collect that money.

Stone filed an immediate appeal. Within a few days, Cates and Ratner stood before an appellate court clerk, waiting to see the appellate court judge assigned for that week to motions in the appellate court. Since the court had begun its summer recess, the appeal could not be heard for months, but Cates was still pressing for a stay of the Departmental hearing. The clerk pointed out to him, however, that he had neglected to attach to his papers a copy of the judgment that he was appealing. Lacking that, Cates could not see an appellate court judge to apply for a stay until the next week.

The next week's judge was Thomas O'Hara, who nine months earlier had sent to the Department of Consumer Affairs a copy of an angry letter of complaint he'd mailed to a collection attorney. The attorney had obtained a judgment against the judge's maid, arising from her installment purchase of a vacuum cleaner. However, she had not received the summons; it was a typical case of what in New York is called "sewer service"—the obtaining of default judgments against debtors on the basis of perjured affidavits of service of process. The attorney had dropped the case in response to the judge's protest. His name was Richard Toole.

Ratner and Cates arrived at the court at 2:00 one day the following week, and the clerks kept them waiting an hour while Judge O'Hara looked at the papers. Then he summoned them to his chambers. Before they could sit down, he announced, "I'm going to deny this application." Cates asked if he could at least argue the point. The judge said that he could, but said he would deny the motion anyway: "Everybody in New York knows about your company," he told Cates. "It's common knowledge."

Cates argued that the Department had unfairly obtained the consent judgment. The judge seemed bored. He interrupted Cates to say, "I know this company. Mr. Richard Toole is involved in sewer service and all kinds of things."

"You see," argued Cates. "That's just why we need the protection of the court. Everyone has a bad impression of the company."

"I can't believe that it's unjustified," said Judge O'Hara. "I know too much about this company."

Cates continued to argue, but to no avail. When he finished, the judge said, "You fellows brought this on yourselves in the way you conducted your sales. The corporation signed the consent judgment and was represented by counsel. Motion denied."

The appellate court's decision was the end of the line. The Department completed its hearing, with Cates still refusing to participate, and revoked Foolproof's license. The banks began to maneuver for position, seeking tactical advantage before the collapse. One of the small banks' attorneys called Ratner to say that Endowment National had misled it into loaning money to Detective by misrepresenting the value of the investment;[10] it wanted to know whether, if it foreclosed and took over collecting the contracts, the Department would raise any objections. Another one urged Ratner to permit the banks to collect from consumers lest banks be deterred from lending to companies selling in low-income areas. "You wouldn't want to frighten banks away from the poor," the bank officer told Ratner. "Foolproof and the banks were working with the ghetto area people."

We began a series of weekly visits to the court, recording the names and addresses of the people Foolproof sued. As soon as Toole filed suit, we sent the defendants a letter advising them of a legal services office willing to represent them. A volunteer lawyer—himself a collection attorney—attached himself to that office and prepared to serve Toole with hundreds of mimeographed answers and demands for pre-trial information, hoping to paralyze Toole's use of the courts to collect Foolproof's debts.

The week I left the Department, a committee of bankers instructed Stone to stop making sales, because selling expenses would reduce the salvage value of the company, and the banks' accountants took up residence in Foolproof's offices to insure that any money coming in from consumers went straight to the banks.

Two weeks later, Foolproof filed a petition in bankruptcy and sought to make what the Bankruptcy Law calls an "arrangement" with its corporate creditors, permitting it to pay its debts to them at an agreed number of cents on the dollar. But Ratner obtained an order from the federal bankruptcy court enabling him to represent thousands of forgotten "creditors"—the consumers who had been gypped over the years and who should stop paying and receive refunds. He won an order permitting any consumer who filed a claim against Foolproof in the bankruptcy court to stop paying the company.

As the company's collapse became total, Ratner was able to convince the Bronx District Attorney's office to intensify its heretofore lackadaisical investigation. In the early autumn of 1971, a Bronx grand jury indicted Stone on thirty-eight counts, including a charge of grand larceny.

The District Attorney announced the indictments in a crowded press conference, with nine television cameras whirring. Edward Thompson, the tough-minded Administrative

Judge of the Civil Court,[11] learned about Stone and his company for the first time through this publicity. On his own, he searched his court's records and discovered that Foolproof had won thousands of default judgments against consumers over a two-year period. On his own motion, he instituted an unprecedented action against Foolproof to reopen all of those judgments, meanwhile staying all of the company's pending suits and its collections on past judgments.

This action, the stay, its consequent cash squeeze, and the attendant publicity forced Stone to negotiate further. On the morning of the hearing on the judge's motion, dozens of low-income consumers, most of them black, filled the judge's anteroom. In his chambers, he hammered out a settlement between Stone, Stone's lawyers, Ratner, the U.S. Attorney, the New York State Attorney General, and the bankruptcy referee; the parties and the referee would set a "fair value" for the alarm, taking into account the aggregate value of all probable consumer defenses. They agreed on $200 after the referee knocked heads together. Consumers would not have to pay more than this amount, and if they had already paid more, they would be entitled to refunds of the excess. Unfortunately, since the banks claimed to have priority in bankruptcy over unsecured creditors, these refunds might never be paid. But at the very least, millions of dollars would be saved for poor consumers. As in the Standard Magazine case, the Department had won mass monetary relief, the novel new remedy provided by the Consumer Protection Law. Yet again these events had come about not through judicial enforcement of that law, but as a result of direct Departmental action.

Cynics sometimes remark that the literature of consumer protection mistakenly focuses on the two-bit chiseler, the ghetto store offering "easy credit" or the fly-by-night door-to-door sales outfit. They argue that government agencies should concentrate instead on the major companies in America, because their mass media advertisements are as deceptive as the sales pitches of the house-to-house peddlers. All advertising, they maintain, is a con.

While there is obviously some truth to their position, I have heard enough fraudulent sales talk by representatives of the commercial underworld to believe that their presentations deserve classification in a separate category—they contain deliberate, unqualified lies and are usually directed to a particularly vulnerable audience, unlike much of the subtly ambiguous falsity of television or magazine advertising.

But the Foolproof case illustrates another way in which major corporations help gyp the American public—not directly, not visibly, but from behind the scenes, by extending mutually profitable lifelines to companies whose business practices they do not wish to know very much about. Foolproof's protectors included a major department store, five banks (including one enormous bank), a prestigious law firm, one of whose partners became a Detective director, an underwriting company, and a public relations securities firm. The company also had a way to generate a telephone call from City Hall.

Any of these institutions could have done some simple investigation of the company before doing business with it. The most cursory glance at the record books open to public inspection in the Civil Court would have revealed that Foolproof was one of the city's most frequent plaintiffs; a few hours' statistical analysis would have demonstrated that of all retailers in the city, Foolproof sued most often. Telephone calls or visits to the company's customers, particularly those customers who had refused to pay, would have revealed that the salesmen were routinely lying, and that the company was violating the door-to-door sales act by not distributing the perforated cards. A company still not convinced that Foolproof was in the business of deception could have spot-checked for itself by asking an employee to request a home visit from a Foolproof salesman. No company made these checks before doing business with Foolproof; they were interested only in making money and then getting out fast when cracks appeared in the ceiling. Each time a major company made a deal with Detective or Foolproof, the prestige of the burglar alarm company increased, so that other large corporations felt "safe" in doing business with it.

No person has observed this process more carefully than Sam Stone. One day, during the negotiations leading to the consent agreement, Stone noticed that a picture frame on my office wall contained an enlargement of a contract form which had once been used by Regal Finance, Inc., the credit company that had financed the sale of Mr. Allen's freezer. Since my battles with it, Regal had abandoned its finance activities in search of other uses of capital.

"What's this doing here?" he asked.

"An earlier lawsuit," I said. "You probably know more about that company than I do."

"Indeed I do," said Stone, evidently eager to talk about a company worse than his. "I know all about them. That company never was more than a stock manipulation."

"How's that?" I asked.

"That company was started by two fellows in the tire business early in the 1960's. They saw a way to make a fast buck. At the time, there were a number of finance companies buying consumer contracts from slum stores. I was President of one of them, as you know. But these contracts were with such poor people, and were subject to so many legal defenses, that no finance company would pay a store more than 75% or 80% of the face value for the right to collect from the consumer. The fellows at Regal decided to pay 97% instead of 75%, and they wiped out the competition.

"Although they knew the paper was uncollectable, they wrote the accounts receivable up on their books for the full face value, and treated those accounts as current income in the year in which the contracts were purchased. That made it look as though the company was very rich, and made it seem as though earnings were skyrocketing. Eventually, the company went public, and people paid a pretty penny for the stock. The owners and directors paid peanuts for their stock, of course.

"The more accounts receivable they had on the books, the more stock they were able to sell. And the more stock they sold, the more the banks and other financial institutions tripped over themselves to lend the company money. The banks were underbidding each other to get Regal to borrow their money. Of course, the banks knew these assets existed only on paper, and that many of them would be uncollectable. But they weren't interested in the contracts as security for the loans. The loans took priority over the stockholders' equity. That equity was their real security. Regal had raised twenty million dollars through the sale of stock, so the banks weren't really worried about losing their money.

"I once offered to lend Regal some money," Stone continued. "The President of the company took me into his office and showed me his financial records. 'These books show that this year I made a million dollars,' he told me.

"But I wasn't so dumb, you know. 'As I read the books,' I said, 'it looks like you lost a million dollars this year.' "

" 'That just shows that you're not living in the jet age, Stone,' he told me. 'On the basis of this statement I was able to sell fourteen million dollars worth of stock. So I lost a million. I still got thirteen million left.'

"The price of Regal Finance kept rising," Stone continued, "and the company's officers and directors kept buying shares at below-market prices. Eventually the company was listed on the American Stock Exchange, and the price went higher. Meanwhile, the company used a variety of accounting techniques to postpone reporting its losses. Finally, in 1969, the bubble broke. The company suddenly announced its discovery that not as much money could be collected on its contracts as had previously been thought. It declared a loss of about twenty million dollars on contracts supposedly worth forty million. Over the course of a few months, the stock plummeted from thirty-four to four. But the insiders sold all the way down. Today some of them are millionaires. The company got out of the finance business, but it had served its purpose.

"The consumers lost out, because Regal then sold their contracts, at a huge discount, to another finance company, which was geared to use even stronger collection techniques than Regal. But the major loss was suffered by the company's innocent stockholders, whose investments were suddenly wiped out. The banks got out all their money, and didn't lose a dime. The only commercial losers were the legitimate finance companies, such as mine, which couldn't meet the competition of the 97% offer, and the low-income retailers, which had no one else to sell their contracts to by the time Regal folded.

"The irony is that food-freezer contracts, the notorious classic case of consumer fraud, made it all possible. The fellows at Regal bought a lot of those contracts in early years, and they never could have gotten the company rolling without them, because each freezer contract had a $1,200 face value. Regal only had to buy 800 contracts to show income of a million dollars."

Our aggressive investigation and direct action against Fool-proof would not have been possible under any but the strongest-willed Commissioner. In this and other cases, the leadership of Bess Myerson was critical. A "political" Commissioner, particularly if he felt insecure as a layman supervising lawyers, would have pulled the reins at half a dozen stages. Commissioner Myerson not only backed us, but urged us on. We discussed with her the pros and cons of mailing the cancellation letter; she analyzed the risks, considered the needs of the low-income victims, and told us to do it. We told her about the call from City Hall, one of several such communications I received in fifteen months in office. She explained, probably correctly, that the Mayor's aides were substantially more jumpy and protective of business than was he, and that they didn't really want to stop her from acting in the public interest, but had to satisfy campaign contributors that they had done something, such as making an inquiry.

She did not allow the call from City Hall to sway our course, either in this or any other investigation. In fact, when she was later invited to appear on the Mayor's weekly television show, she used the occasion to inform the public about Foolproof, though the station blipped the name of the company from the sound track of the television tape.

We were awed by her gutsiness and her intuitive sense of when a plan or strategy would work and when it was inappropriate. Yet this was a quality that the public, at least the intellectual public, appeared to know nothing about. Acquaintances would always ask us: "You work for Bess Myerson? Is she really smart?" Nothing was more galling, more embarrassing, than to be introduced, privately or publicly, as "the brains behind Bess Myerson," yet such was the tag attributed, from time to time, to all of the lawyers in the office.

Almost all of our adversaries, from the "discount" appliance stores on the Lower East Side to the $100,000 a year lawyers on Wall Street, assumed that they were being hounded by some over-zealous adolescents, and that an appeal to Commissioner Myerson would ease the pressure. They called her by day and by night, at her home and her office; they approached her directly and through intermediaries who knew her personally. She avoided their calls if she could. If she could not, she told them politely and firmly that her staff spoke for her, and that she never interfered in a case at the behest of one of the Department's respondents.

And she never did.

NOTES

1. We later learned that Foolproof salesmen carried police radios in their cars and cruised to the site of a burglary.

2. Here, too, the size and reputation of the company are a significant part of the tale, but so is the secrecy surrounding its name. The reader must take my word for it that "Bramson's" reputation is comparable with that of J. C. Penney's—a name I can safely use by way of illustration since Penney's, with no New York City outlet, cannot be Bramson's.

3. N. Y. Pers. Prop. Law art. 10(a) (1970).

4. "To Foolproof Protection, Inc.: One of your salesmen sold me a burglar alarm and installation and maintenance services at my home after September 1, 1970. At no time did you inform me of my right to cancel under New York Personal Property Law, Sections 425–430. I now cancel. Within ten days send me the agreement I signed and all the money I paid you. My name and address is:————"

5. He got it; Ratner is now the City's Consumer Advocate.

6. *The Amsterdam News,* New York's major black newspaper, did not pick up the story until two months later, when it suddenly printed the press release in full.

7. A motion without notice can be made in any county. CPLR Section 2212(b).

8. "That branch of the motion which seeks to vacate and set aside or modify the consent judgment is denied. To vacate the judgment herein the burden is upon the movants to show fraud, coercion or misrepresentation. Defendants have made no such credible showing. The defendants knowingly and intentionally entered into a legal and binding agreement. They were represented by counsel and had adequate opportunity to refuse to the entry of the consent judgment. [As for the license hearing,] the hearing is not in excess of the Department's authority or jurisdiction nor can this court assume that the hearing will be unreasonable, biased or unfair. Lastly, defendants will have an adequate remedy for judicial review in the event the hearing is adverse to their interests."

9. I have tried to discover the purpose of this arrangement. Under federal law, banks are not permitted to have more than a fixed percentage of their assets loaned to risky enterprises. They are not supposed to know in advance the schedules of the bank examiners. But might they be so arranging their loans so as to have less money in risky ventures in the months when they will be examined?

10. The small bank could theoretically sue Endowment for damages caused by any misrepresentation, but this course was practically foreclosed to it, the lawyer said, because small banks thrive on referrals of business by big banks, and a small bank that acted uppity by suing a big bank would be blackballed in the banking community.

11. The Civil Court is the court in which companies sue to collect on installment contracts. The Department could not bring suit under the Consumer Protection Law before Judge Thompson, or in his court, because that court lacks equitable jurisdiction. N. Y. Civil Court Act, § 202 (McKinney's 1963).

8 · Ethics: The Case of the Secret Agent

THE CASE THAT prompted us, during the spring of 1971, to evaluate our own feelings about our investigative tactics came to us from a salesgirl who resigned in disgust from Superior Research Enterprises, Inc. She called us to report that the relatively new company, for which she had worked only briefly, sold cheap books for a great deal of money, door-to-door. Among other misleading tactics, she said, the company instructed its salesgirls to mislead buyers to believe that it was connected with the famous children's television show, "Sesame Street."

She had gone to work for the company, she told us, after responding to an advertisement for "interviewers" in the *Village Voice*, a popular New York newspaper. The advertisement had not revealed that the job was basically selling.

Then she had been instructed in "cold canvassing"—selling door-to-door without previous appointment—as practiced by the company. Using a new "Sesame Street" album as an entrée, she was to determine whether the home had children; if so, to engage the mother of the house in conversation, ask a series of survey questions, and then discuss the company's program, in which the mother could enroll. Then she was to talk the mother into signing a contract for materials to be delivered at a later date, which our informant felt were virtually worthless.

Another young girl, who had recently left the company, called with a similar story a few days later. Although we had not received any complaints from the company's consumers, we judged that this might be the beginning of a fraudulent plan that would later generate many complaints—possibly when the company began suing people who didn't pay. We decided to investigate the company at a time when we might prevent trouble, rather than waiting for hundreds of people to be swindled.

Our immediate problem was that neither girl could remember exactly what she had been told to tell the mothers, and we had no mothers reporting what had been said to them. We wanted an accurate statement of what was said, to corroborate the girls, and to give us evidence for any subsequent proceeding.

We could have issued a subpoena and requested the company's President to tell us what his employees' sales pitch was, but we knew that he could postpone any hearing for months through a variety of delaying tactics, and that when he finally testified he might deny knowledge of what the salesgirls said or might tone down or color the presentation for our benefit.

To get a fast, accurate record, we decided to do what we had done so successfully in the Standard Magazine case—get one of our own employees a job working for the company.

It was Sylvia Kronstadt's first case, but we knew that she could do the job. Twenty-one years old, she was about to graduate from the University of Utah with every honor known to that school. She was at the top of her class, had participated in dozens of organizational activities and, as community affairs editor of the school newspaper, had snowed us with the investigative exposés she'd written about the University's complicity in chemical warfare research, migrant labor in Utah, and other controversial subjects. She had somehow read about the Law Enforcement Division in a western newspaper, and had wandered to New York to seek a job with us as an investigator while completing her last semester by remote control. She also bore the features and physical attributes suggested by numerous movies as desirable characteristics for a female secret agent.

She answered the *Village Voice* advertisement, and was asked to come for an interview with the company's President, Ron Lumak. She packed a tape recorder in her pocketbook.

Lumak turned out to be younger than she'd expected, short, and very nervous. He talked quickly, while she completed the job application. He was looking, he told her, for young women who were creative, and who had a social conscience—women who, additionally, wanted a creative rather than a hum-drum job. Selling the company's services, he said, requires creativity because every mother is different. "You have to use a different psychology on each one."

Although his company was only a year old, Lumak told Kronstadt, it already had 90,000 subscribers in New York. He employed about sixty salesgirls, who were given a one-day training session. After that, they were driven each day by a "crew manager" to a lower middle-class residential area of the city, where they sold a package of educational materials produced by a company in Chicago.

The interview lasted forty-five minutes. Kronstadt drew upon her true background, omitting only the week she'd worked with the Department, and impressed him as strongly as she'd impressed us. Lumak offered her a job selling the company's services. "But," he said, "you really are smart. Wouldn't you rather work as my special assistant here in the office, training salesgirls, interviewing candidates, and working on the business records?"

Kronstadt drew a breath, and thought for a moment. "I might," she said, "but first I'd like to try working in the field, to get a better feel for the organization. Perhaps after a day

or two of that I could consider working here in the office."
He suggested that she attend a training session the next day,
and she accepted, with a new cassette in her recorder.

The trainer was a young woman, Delores West, who had
worked for the company since its start. She outlined the
official sales presentation to her trainees. "Hi," it began, "my
name is ————. I'm with Superior Research, and we're
speaking to all the mothers in the neighborhood about the
new 'Sesame Street' album. We've made it part of our child
development program for young children. Do you mind if I
ask you a few questions about your opinion on education?"

Then the salesgirl was to request entry into the home so
that she could use a table to write down the answers. "Which
do you feel are the most impressionable years in a person's
life—childhood, adolescence, or adulthood? Which institution had the greatest impact—home, school, or church?
What type of employment is your husband in?" No sales
were to be made to the unemployed who had no salaries to
garnishee.

The salesgirls were instructed to pretend to record the answers to the questions, and then to ask: "Are you familiar
with the work of the Children's Educational Workshop?[1]
Well, how about Project Head Start? As you know, poor people have Head Start to give them an educational advantage,
and the rich have private schools, but the middle-class
mother felt left out and wanted to have a program that
would provide her children with the same opportunities that
other children were receiving."

The salesgirl was then to list the "offerings" of the
"Workshop":

> (1) A "10–year information service," to which children could
> direct "any questions" and receive two-to-twenty page re-
> search reports. (The service is run by a Chicago company,
> which maintains thousands of files responding to questions
> children frequently ask; copies of the prepackaged reports in
> the files are sent to subscribing families who have purchased
> the service through hundreds of companies like Superior Re-

search located throughout the country.) Delores West explained how to make mothers feel the need for the information service: "get the parent off-balance and insecure" by showing them examples of the "new math"; make them feel that they cannot communicate with their children about their education. If the mother objected that her children were too young to use the information service effectively, the salesgirls were to refer to a Harvard experiment in which a 5-month-old child's IQ was increased 14 points in 3 months.

(2) Four pamphlets on child guidance, including articles on thumb sucking, bed wetting, and stealing. The salesgirls were to show the mothers a poster illustrating these pamphlets. A banner heading on the poster read "YOUR MOTHERS CLUB," as if the mothers were being asked to join something rather than buy something.

(3) A fifteen to thirty-five percent discount on purchases of products contained in a color catalog. "Flip through the catalog, and let the mother see the pictures," said West, "but never let her pick it up or examine it." The catalog bore no address, publisher's name, or other indication of origin, and contained no price list.

(4) "an exclusive option" to buy an Annual Events Book every year, for six dollars.

(5) a "Career guidance chart" (consisting of one page, with arrows pointing from interests to jobs. The chart indicated, for example, that a child interested in gardening might have a career ahead in the civil service.)

(6) The right to purchase "educational materials" from the company for half-price. No further details of this were given the salesgirls.

The girls were then to say, "Now, because of the new methods of teaching, we're trying to enroll more mothers in our program. We are currently giving premium inducements for joining the club." It was illegal, Miss West explained, to say that anything was free, so the girls should use this phrasing so that the mother would "get that impression anyway."

The items designated as "premium inducements"—a

168]   COUNSEL FOR THE DECEIVED

twelve-volume set of children's books, a seven-volume science library, a dictionary, the "Sesame Street" record album, and two posters—were the only materials of any significant value; the mothers were supposed to see this while suspecting that the salesgirls didn't, which would make the mothers feel that they were taking advantage of the program.

"To close the sale," instructed West, "just assume that the mother wants to join, and breeze right into closure. Never ask her to 'sign' anything. Get her signature by telling her to 'write down your name for the office' or say, 'just O.K. this application here.' Don't tell them that the form is a contract, and don't tell them the total price. If they ask, tell them that it only costs eighty-nine cents per week, but don't tell them that they will have to pay for 297 weeks.

"If the mother appears hesitant after learning the price," West continued, "say, 'Aren't you strong enough as a mother to put away eighty-nine cents a week for your child's education?'

"After the mother has signed, tell her that the 'delivery boy' will be in the area the next day to bring the books, and ask her whether morning or evening is most convenient. Say that the program used to mail the books, but that they were stolen half the time, so that you now use your own delivery boys. It's important that the mother be home when the delivery boy comes, because he's the real salesman. He signs the mother up on a contract to pay at the rate of about ten dollars a month, and gives her a discount for her agreement to pay at this accelerated rate.

"Incidentally, here's a little hint to improve your selling success. Make up a few names and write them at the top of your enrollment sheet, so that it will look like everyone in the neighborhood is joining. And don't worry if your presentation isn't perfect for a few days. These people never ask questions anyway, and most of them are so dumb they don't know if what you're saying is right or not."

Lumak had been sitting at the side of the room. Now he broke in, "The secret is to get them so hypnotized by your presentation that they don't know what hit them. And re-member, in dealing with the consumer, people like us have to come down a few notches."

The next day, Kronstadt was taken out in the field to make sales by a man named Larry Williams, an officer of the company. Delores West went with them. They drove to Queens, where they met a man named Mike and a salesgirl named Rose. Mike was a crew leader, a position he'd held in companies doing this type of selling all over the country. He selected a neighborhood for the day's canvassing. During the ride, Rose gave Sylvia Kronstadt a few more hints.

"Play on the mother's sympathy," she advised. "You're this poor, hardworking young girl, trudging around in the rain or the heat, just trying to make an honest living. They love you—they sit you down and make you coffee, and you've got them in the palm of your hand. It's all very woman to woman, and easy to clinch sales.

"What's bad is when you get into an area where the people are pretty educated and they start asking you ques-tions. When you hit a block like that, forget it—they're too smart."

"Delores, can I watch you make a presentation before I try it?" asked Kronstadt. "I don't feel comfortable doing it alone."

"I'm sure you can do it alone, Sylvia. It's not hard."

"Please?"

Delores West relented, and agreed to give Kronstadt a demonstration. "I didn't want to demonstrate for you," she said, "because the way I do it is illegal. If there are only a few doing it this way, we don't get caught. But if I teach people to do it this way, we'll probably get caught." The tape re-corder whirred away in Kronstadt's bag.

The car stopped in an Italian neighborhood. Kronstadt went with Delores West; the others fanned out. It took them twenty-five minutes before they found a mother who spoke English. When they did, West asked her if they might ask a "few questions from Superior Research" about her opinions.

"Are you selling something?" asked the woman.

"Oh, no," said West. "We're just interviewing mothers about their views on education."

The woman admitted them to her house, which consisted of several small, cramped rooms. Her six children scampered in and out as Delores West explained the services of the "club" and invited her to join. The woman said very little, and finally signed the contract.

Outside, West turned to Kronstadt. "Wasn't that awful?" she asked. "I almost feel bad about that one. She was so stupid she would have bought anything from anyone."

Kronstadt then left West, ostensibly to do her own canvassing. However, she instead returned to Manhattan and telephoned Ron Lumak, to accept his offer to be his special assistant. He told her to report for work the following Monday.

On her first day in the office, Lumak trained her. "The key word in this job is control," he told her. "*We* are in control, and we must remain in control. We don't ask people, we tell them. And we tell them what we want them to know, when we want them to know it. The psychology of this job is to never let anyone get that control from you.

"Control is all important. Everything I ever say professionally is prepared in advance and memorized, including gestures, even laughs. From now on, write down everything I do, and memorize it.

"When a job applicant calls, don't answer her questions. Just say that the job involves field work, interviewing mothers in their homes about a new educational program for their children, to see if they qualify. If they ask any questions, say that Ron will kill you if you talk about it. Say that he likes to tell them about it himself."

"How do the applicants learn about sales jobs?" Kronstadt asked.

"We run two ads a week, in the *Village Voice* and the *New York Times*," Lumak replied. "The Civil Rights Law says we can't discriminate, so we have to solicit both male and female interviewers. If a man calls, just tell him that the position is filled."

"How many salesgirls do you want to have?"

"There is no ceiling. The summer months are a peak period, with college girls home for the summer. In June and July we could interview up to a hundred girls a day for jobs. That's the main thing I want you to do for now, concentrate on recruiting salesgirls. When you interview them, use the interview script exactly. I've worked it out in detail, and every word has a purpose. And weed out the ones who ask a lot of questions. If you get just one person like that into a training session, they can ruin the whole thing—they can plant a seed of doubt or suspicion in everyone's mind."

Kronstadt worked for Lumak for three days. For her, they were days of intense emotional ambivalence. She knew the company was cheating its customers, and believed in her real work, which was to document it. But at the same time, she was most unhappy in her undercover role. Lumak was talking to her out of trust; he already had a genuinely warm feeling toward his new protégé. As time passed, Lumak, West, and Kronstadt exchanged the small talk—about painting the offices, what to have to lunch, their careers—on which office friendships are built. Lumak told Kronstadt of his background, and she began to sympathize with him, to lose her capacity for blame. He had come from an immigrant background, and his hopes for self-improvement had been dashed again and again. He had come to believe that the only way to get ahead was over the backs of others.

Toward evening the second day, Lumak was sitting a few feet from Kronstadt, but facing away from her. Her telephone rang. Calling from the next desk, Lumak asked her to dinner, and she declined. During the conversation, he never once turned to look at her.

She was left alone in the office for hours at a time. At first with hesitation, then more confidently, she perused the company's files. She learned the structure of the business, the types of forms it used. She copied the names and addresses of its supply sources for books and services. She found in the files an out-of-court settlement which Lumak had signed with the State Attorney General the previous year, on behalf of a similar but differently named company; in it he had agreed not to falsely describe the sales jobs for which his company sought applicants. She found the financial records, and calculated that all of the goods and services, for which the customer was charged $264.33, cost the company only $38. The ten-year information service, for instance, cost the company a dollar per subscriber.

She obtained the names of some subscribers from the files, so that she could contact them to determine whether they had complaints. But their dates of purchase were a year earlier, when Lumak had a different company. She really needed the names of the current customers, and those Lumak kept in the top drawer of his own desk.

As it was, she was frightened about rummaging through the files. She would take a document to her desk to read, but then she would hear a muffled sound in the corridor outside, and quickly run back to the file cabinet to return the document. She couldn't bring herself to go through Lumak's desk.

On the third day, as she was alone in the office, studying the company's forms, she suddenly looked up to find a young man, about eighteen years old, who had silently entered the room and was watching her.

She collected herself. "Can I help you?" she asked calmly.

Equally calmly, he replied, "No, that's O.K., I'll just take this." He picked up her pocketbook (that day, without recorder), and ran from the building. She had lost forty dollars.

The next morning, Kronstadt had Newman call Lumak to say that she would not be in—that day or in the future. Newman said he was a friend, calling with the message that she had enjoyed the job, but that she had to quit to visit her dying grandmother in North Carolina. But later that day, the superintendent of the building next door to Superior's offices called Kronstadt's own superintendent to say that he had found her wallet, with his telephone number on a scrap of paper inside. She went to retrieve her wallet and identification cards—the money was gone. Unknown to her, as she passed Superior's building, Lumak was watching her from his window.

Now Lumak became suspicious. He called her father at her home in Utah, and spoke to her mother. "This is Sylvia's employer, Ron Lumak," he said. "She isn't in today because of a sickness in your family. But I have to reach her right away. Can you tell me who in the family is sick?"

Not only did the Department's investigators have to be sharp; they had to have clever mothers. Mrs. Kronstadt knew that her daughter worked for the Department but had no notion of her secret role; yet when Lumak called, she reacted smoothly. She said that her daughter did have a sick grandmother in North Carolina.

"What's the telephone number there?" Lumak asked.

"I don't have it," said Mrs. Kronstadt, beginning to become suspicious.

"Isn't it odd that you don't have your mother's telephone number?" Lumak challenged her.

"Oh it's not my mother," said Mrs. Kronstadt. "It's my husband's mother. But he's not here. He's at his office."

"I see. Can you give me his office telephone number?"

"Surely," she said, and gave it to him.

As soon as Lumak hung up, Mrs. Kronstadt dialed her husband. She reached him seconds before Lumak did, and on her advice, Mr. Kronstadt told his secretary to say that he was out of the office and would not return for several hours. Then he called his daughter at the Department, and was briefed on her assignment.

When Lumak called that afternoon to ask for the telephone number, Mr. Kronstadt told him that Sylvia's grandmother lived in Fuquay-Varina, a town so small that telephone service had not yet been installed.

"Incidentally, Mr. Kronstadt, is it your mother or Mrs. Kronstadt's mother who is ill?"

"It's Mrs. Kronstadt's mother," he said.

Lumak pounced. "But Mrs. Kronstadt told me that it was your mother!"

"It really is Mrs. Kronstadt's mother," said Mr. Kronstadt coolly. "But Mrs. Kronstadt is ill herself, and we didn't want to worry her by telling her that her mother was dying. So we've told her that my mother was the one who was sick."

Back in New York, Lumak pondered on the likelihood that both of Sylvia Kronstadt's grandmothers lived in Fuquay-Varina, North Carolina.

That evening, Kronstadt was working on a case at her home with Dennis Grossman, another Department lawyer. Her studio apartment was in a six-floor elevator building on a quiet street in mid-town Manhattan. Since, at that time, she was still a relatively new arrival in New York, the telephone company had not yet come to install a phone. At 11:30, Grossman left the apartment and rode downstairs in the elevator. As he opened the inside lobby door, he saw two young men studying the names listed on the building's intercom system. From Kronstadt's description, he instantly recognized them as Ron Lumak and Larry Williams. They spotted him at the same time that he saw them, and Williams grabbed the door that Grossman had just opened. Grossman blocked the entrance with his body.

"Does Sylvia Kronstadt live here?" Lumak asked. "She's not listed on the buzzers."

"I don't know," said Grossman. "I never heard of her."

Both men shoved past Grossman at once, into the apartment lobby.

"Hey, you can't do that," he called. "You can't go upstairs unless a tenant buzzes you up."

"Let's start on the sixth floor and work our way down," Williams said to Lumak.

The two men got into the elevator cab, and as it began its ascent, Grossman ran up five flights of stairs, possibly setting a world speed record for that feat. As he stood outside her apartment, his heart pounding both from his run and from fear, he could hear the men knocking on apartment doors on the floor above and asking for her. He could not hear the tenants' responses. He knocked rapidly but quietly on her door, and she opened it.

Grossman rushed into the room and closed and locked the door behind him. Before a bewildered Sylvia Kronstadt, he turned off the radio, doused the lights, and whispered, "Don't say a word!"

Instantly, there was a banging on her door. Grossman and Kronstadt stood silently, not moving, as the noise continued. When she heard the voice of her caller, she understood.

"Sylvia," yelled Lumak. "We know you're in there. Let us in."

They made no response. The banging continued.

For twenty minutes, Grossman and Kronstadt stood frozen, while Lumak and Williams alternately banged on the door and listened for a response. Having no telephone Kronstadt could not call the police. Finally, there was a long period of silence, and it seemed that the intruders had left. Kronstadt tiptoed to the door to peer through the peephole. As she neared it, a floorboard creaked.

The banging resumed immediately. "Now we're sure that you're inside," called Lumak.

Twenty minutes longer the banging continued. Finally it stopped. An upstairs neighbor had summoned the police because she could not sleep. Lumak explained that the person they wanted to visit seemed not to be at home, so the men and the police left without speaking to Kronstadt. She sent Grossman home and went to sleep.

At three o'clock in the morning she was awakened by the ringing of her intercom buzzer. She did not answer it, and it continued to ring intermittently for an hour. When it stopped at four, she went back to bed.

As she was leaving for work that morning, a neighbor

stopped her in the vestibule. "Say, two fellows were looking for you this morning, about half an hour ago. Did they find you?"

That day, Henry Stern called Ron Lumak and informed him that Sylvia Kronstadt was an investigator for the Department of Consumer Affairs, and that while Lumak might be excused for harassing her before he knew her mission, the Department expected that he would refrain, from that point on, from any further contact with her. Lumak was speechless. He had not memorized a script for this occasion. The undercover phase of our investigation was at an end.

The case was now at a critical juncture; we had to decide whether to follow a judicial or a direct action strategy. We would undoubtedly have selected a direct action strategy without prolonged deliberation had not our doubts about our own methods during the investigative stage provoked a more searching inquiry.

We had to face the fact that more than ever before, the use of unorthodox methods had led to a situation where we believed that an employee's life may have been in danger. Was it worth it? Did the company's deception of its customers and its contempt for them justify the actions we had taken, and more particularly, did they justify further direct action on our part? While we had become cynical about stopping fraud by going to court, who were we to use other methods, at physical risk to the young men and women of the Division, if society did not care to provide the instruments for dealing with such matters in a judicial forum?

Before making the inevitable strategic and ethical judgment, we considered the specific tactics that we might employ. If we chose the judicial route, we would have to start by trying to subpoena records of recent sales. We could never get a preliminary injunction without consumer affidavits. Yet despite the most extensive undercover work we'd ever engaged in, one that had revealed a serious pattern of consumer fraud, we still had no consumer complaints nor even the names of consumers who had recently purchased materials.

The company was not yet suing people, so names of parties could not be culled from court records. They would have to come from the company itself, which we knew would be beginning an intensive summer selling season in a few weeks. If Lumak chose to fight the subpoena in court, he would probably lose, but could avoid giving us the documents until fall at the earliest, and by appealing, until winter or the following spring. Then it would take more months before we could obtain the necessary affidavits and present the case to the court for decision.

We listed the possible alternatives for direct action. The company obtained salesgirls by advertising in the *Village Voice* and the *New York Times*. We could inform those media of what we had learned, and they might refuse to carry further advertising.

We could issue a press release about what we had found out about the company. That was unlikely to be effective; people do not remember the names of companies they are warned to look out for, and if they did, Lumak could change the company's name. Furthermore, newspapers in New York, we had found, did not devote substantial space to stories of consumer fraud unless a big-name company was involved (and sometimes not even then), or unless the Department took unusual measures to indicate to the press the importance of the story.

We considered holding a public hearing. At such a session, we could play our tape recordings, and the result might be sensational, producing more prominent newspaper stories than would a mere press release. But even assuming that people would remember these stories, what were we to make of the charge, frequently hurled at the Department by businesses it attacks, and certain to be made by Superior, that we were "trying the case in the press rather than in the courts?" Did this slogan speak to an important ethical principle deeply rooted in the American legal system, and therefore to be respected, or was it merely the standard reflex reaction of those whose actions cannot withstand public scrutiny to a tactic which has been used by government, with at least tacit support from the public, from time immemorial?

We also considered, at least in conversation, even more unorthodox approaches. Would it be improper, we wondered, for Department employees, such as paraprofessionals, to picket Lumak's offices, carrying signs explaining what the company did? If that was going too far, or even if it were merely an inefficient use of Department resources, it might be possible for the paraprofessionals to organize a genuine community action group to picket this and other companies regularly. Was that a legitimate government function? What about picketing Lumak's house in Brooklyn, so that his neighbors would know the type of business in which he engaged? Was that any less proper than publicizing his activities in the newspaper? Picketing businessmen's homes had been done by community groups protesting real estate block busters. Was it unethical for the government to participate?

We recalled, also, that Lumak had told Kronstadt that a single person who announced her qualms during a training session could cause dissension in an entire group. It occurred to us that we might send an employee, or a volunteer, to each one of his training sessions, by flooding him with job applications; the agent would ask questions such as "Isn't it wrong to lie to people?" in an effort to encourage all the others to evaluate their own participation. Was this wrong? And we considered organizing a "truth squad" to follow his salesgirls around in the neighborhoods, telling each mother how much the company's products really cost, and that the company was a commercial venture unrelated to "Sesame Street," any survey organization, or any real research project. Finally, we considered attacking one of Superior's few visible synapses by informing the company's suppliers of its activities, and suggesting to them that we might have to investigate whether fraudulent use of their products, with their knowledge, by their customer, involved them in any violation of law.

All of these tactics had to be measured against invocation of the judicial system, and we had nothing but our suspicions to support our feeling that Lumak would use all available delaying tactics to oppose us in court.

Before committing ourselves to either a judicial or a direct action strategy, we put a toe in each pond. On May 21, 1971, we served a subpoena on Lumak and, as expected, he retained Cates, who began a classic, long drawn-out court battle to challenge its validity. We also put pressure on a corporate synapse by informing the *Village Voice* and the *New York Times* that the "interviewer" positions for which the company was advertising were really sales jobs, and we told those newspapers what we had learned about the company's sales methods. The *Voice* stopped accepting the advertising; the *Times* transferred it to the "Sales Help Wanted" column. This did not appreciably reduce the number of girls who sought jobs from Superior Research, so that when I left, the Department was faced with a pressing strategic question which the case would force it to resolve.

After I left the agency, my successor, Bruce Ratner, adopted an essentially judicial approach to the case: he decided to suspend direct pressure while seeking judicial enforcement of its May subpoena. The company's motion to quash was submitted to the court early in June. Late in July, the court ruled in favor of the Department. But then the judge went on a month's vacation, so it was impossible for Ratner to submit an order for him to sign, which could be served on the company. When the judge returned early in September, Ratner mailed his proposed order to the court. For three weeks, he heard nothing. Then he called the clerk. The clerk could not find the order.

The next week, the clerk found the proposed order and mailed it back to Ratner, unsigned; Ratner's draft was defective in several formal respects. For example, the word "enter" above the line for the judge's signature was on the right of the page, instead of being centered.

Ratner submitted a new draft, which the judge signed at the end of September. Ratner served the order on the company, demanding a hearing in early October.

On the hearing date, a new lawyer for the company appeared at the Department, demanding a week's postponement so that he could familiarize himself with the case. Reluctantly, Ratner gave him a week. During that time, the company appealed the decision against it, and the appellate court stayed the hearing pending appeal. The appeal was scheduled for early December; a decision might be expected early the next year. If the Department's position were sustained, and the company chose not to appeal further, the Law Enforcement Division could begin its investigation. Meanwhile, the summer home solicitation selling season, which Lumak had told Kronstadt would be the company's most successful period, had long since come and gone.

The lawyers of the Law Enforcement Division often debated the ethics of our investigative and enforcement techniques; the Superior Research case sharpened our questioning and caused us to wonder about how the police must feel. If *we* could feel the courts driving us out of the normal channels into a kind of street warfare, we imagined that the police must feel the pressure a hundredfold.

All of us in the Law Enforcement Division were civil libertarians. We applauded the Supreme Court decision requiring policemen to warn suspects that their admissions could be used against them, and scoffed at police officials who claimed that the case would "hamstring" law enforcement officials. We condemned eavesdropping and wiretapping. We decried the loss of privacy in American life. We demonstrated when police forces took the law into their own hands and beat kids over the head, or when they stood by passively while construction workers did so. We protested the use of informers and secret agents to convict Jimmy Hoffa.

Yet here we were, after submitting for only one year to

the frustrations of law enforcement, eager to emulate every police trick we despised, and indeed, ready to invent a few of our own. By the end of that year we had an impressive inventory of electronic gadgetry, including a subminiature tape recorder with one microphone that looked like a vest-pocket fountain pen and another that hooked onto a bra-strap. (One hazard of a very young law enforcement staff: on the day this microphone was to be used for the first time, our investigator forgot to wear a bra.) We thought of the press as one of a number of arrows for our bow, rather than the safeguard of a free people against oppressive government. We first learned that the government had to lie when we discovered that many subpoenas could not be served unless we used a ruse to get into the presence of a company's officers; by the end of the year, we were routinely engaging in deception to fight deception, and even the use of wired secret agents to infiltrate companies was becoming commonplace.

A lunch-table conversation revealed that all of us were horrified at J. Edgar Hoover's pre-trial release to the press of the alleged correspondence between Father Berrigan and Sister McAlister concerning the possible kidnapping of Henry Kissinger. Was that public statement so different from the public hearing we were considering for Superior Research? We regarded blacklisting of film artists during the McCarthy era as one of the darkest hours of the Constitution; was it so different from our sometimes subtle, sometimes not-so-subtle hints to newspapers, magazines, banks, stores, and other institutions that one of their customers was cheating people, although no court had so determined? We feared the advent of a national data bank, a computer in Washington with dossiers on every American, culled from the records of every local, state, and federal agency with which a person had contact from birth to death. Yet we encouraged and actively participated in the creation of a consumer complaint data bank, now being assembled in a computer in Washington by the Federal Trade Commission, in which are recorded the details of every complaint about a company made to every consumer protection agency in the country, including, of course, the company's name.

What was enforcing the law—which ought to be a matter of some pride—doing to us? After her service as a secret agent, Sylvia Kronstadt told me, "I haven't resolved it myself. I'm not proud at all of having done that, and I'm not proud to admit to the people who pay me, the citizens, that I've done that. But I think Lumak is a crook."

We were driven to direct action, and to use unpleasant investigative techniques, by sympathy with the victims of consumer fraud and by what we regarded as a breakdown in the system of civil justice. But what policemen experience is much worse, in both respects. We talked, day by day, with people who had been gypped out of a few dozen or a few hundred dollars. Their stories enraged us. The police, by contrast, see the victims of physical violence—people who have been robbed, shot, and raped; they often talk to victims of crime who are still shaking with fright. Contact with these persons must anger the young policeman, must create in him a determination to apprehend and punish the offender, one way or another. And when he turns to the courts, he discovers that the system of criminal justice has failed more completely than the system of civil justice. When a man is released on bail, and fails to appear for trial, his bail is forfeited, and a bench warrant is issued for his arrest, but I have heard that in New York City, only two out of seven of such warrants are ever executed. The failures of the correctional system produce much public talk but little willingness to spend money for improvement; the recidivism rate climbs higher. And, perhaps, the decisions of the courts do make it harder to convict the guilty; I am quite certain that fewer of the businessmen we interrogated would have cooperated if we had started their hearings with the *Miranda* warnings that must be given criminal suspects.

Of course, there are differences between the steps we took and the actions we condemn the police and the FBI for taking. We were dealing with companies, not individuals. And most of the ethically debatable measures we took were neither specifically permitted nor specifically prohibited by law, while, for example, beating up an almost certainly guilty rapist whom the courts, applying strict rules of evidence, would not convict, is clearly illegal. But these distinctions go only so far. Some corporations—such as Wondra—are basically the creation and embodiment of one individual; indeed, some companies are not corporations at all, but partnerships or individual proprietorships. To strike at these companies is really to strike at the earning power of the individuals behind them, and if the strike is successfully done by publicity, it does seem a little like blacklisting a professional. Surely, avoiding specifically illegal actions does not free a public agency to do anything else it pleases; its actions must be related to its mission.

But what is an agency's mission? How broadly or narrowly do we define its powers when we, the public, create an institution? The question cannot be answered by consulting the people who wrote the statute; I wrote the Consumer Protection Law, from the first draft to the final version collated on the floor of the City Council, and while I can offer a good deal of advice on what business conduct it permits and prohibits, I have no idea what *agency* conduct it permits or prohibits. Nor are the critics of the statute-writers much help. I told a seminar of law professors about the Department's activities in the Foolproof case, and the responses ranged from general approval—"that's exactly what government agencies should be doing"—to general condemnation.

Obviously, the puzzle should be avoided rather than solved; we should streamline and liberalize the law enforcement process so that backlogs are eliminated, delay made impossible, bureaucracy suppressed, and judges sensitized to justice. Meanwhile, conscientious law enforcement agencies will continue to be stretched between their concepts of service and their devotion to the judicial system. It's a hell of a choice to have to make.

NOTES

1. Children's *Television* Workshop is the producer of "Sesame Street."

9 · Beyond
Law Enforcement

MY DEPARTURE from the Department of Consumer Affairs was not a resignation of protest but one of disappointment. Although the Commissioner and the city had given the Law Enforcement Division all the political, financial, and legal support that could reasonably be asked (given New York City's proximity to municipal bankruptcy), we were having little discernible impact on the level of consumer fraud in New York.

To be sure, no one would again be deceived by Foolproof Protection, or by any of a dozen major frauds that folded their fine-print contracts as a result of our investigation and action. But at one time during the drafting of the Consumer Protection Law, I had actually imagined that a good law, properly administered, could wipe out misleading sales practices altogether. Our experiences shed little light on whether enough law enforcement could ever do the job, but they do suggest that given our toleration of the way in which adversary and judicial systems now operate, the amount of resources constituting "enough" would be more than any government should devote to the problem.

In my imaginary model of how the new law would work, I had made several erroneous assumptions. The first was that people would know when they were gypped. However, whole classes of transactions in violation of the Consumer Protection Law never came to our attention because some frauds are so successful that they do not generate complaints. For example, although courses and correspondence lessons in the occult and the attainment of psychic powers are frequently advertised in magazines with high circulation among New York's low-income population, we never had a single complaint from a disappointed purchaser. A chain-letter franchising plan that was the subject of a Federal Trade Commission proceeding moved into New York but came to our attention only because one of our lawyers was approached to join; the victims saw no reason to complain because even after they learned the government's allegations, they thought they could make money by selling further franchises to expand the chain.

Second, I had assumed that once the law was in operation, every consumer who knew he had a problem would complain to the Department. But many New Yorkers—probably most—did not know of the Department's complaint service, and a large segment of those who knew of it did not use it. Media appearances or public service announcements by the Commissioner generally produced a flood of complaints, but, naturally, most of them were trivial in nature, such as complaints that a grocery store was carrying wilted lettuce; the main effect of the media-generated complaints was to create a backlog in complaint processing, which then discouraged Commissioner Myerson from making further public appeals. It proved impossible to broadcast selective appeals for the types of complaints that the Department had the legal power to resolve. More seriously, few complaints came from the low-income areas of the city, where the most serious frauds were perpetrated; whether out of lack of information about the Department, cynicism about its effectiveness, or preoccupation with other types of problems, minority group victims rarely brought us their grievances.

Third, I had incorrectly estimated the amount of time

and manpower that the resolution of each case would require. The delays and obstructions I had experienced in the Allen case were, to my surprise, equally visited on public law enforcers; in fact, to the extent that government had to cope with internal, bureaucratic sources of delay, its problems were magnified. Only when we avoided going to court were we able to achieve results before the complainants forgot that they had complained.

Finally, I had grossly misunderstood the dynamics of the enforcement system. I had imagined that as we successfully sued companies, word of our aggressive stance would spread among those committing deception, and that therefore, in most cases, we would be able to achieve refunds merely by making a telephone call. In those cases where a telephone call would not suffice, we would promptly investigate and sue, and under the statute, consumers would then be reimbursed for the time they spent pursuing their complaints. In addition, the Department would recover its costs of investigation, and in mass restitution cases, would, under the law, profit by the amount of money recovered which was not distributed to consumers who could not be located. The law was supposed to generate a system of positive feedback, in which the Department would actually enlarge itself by bringing big cases.

During my term of office, those novel statutory provisions never came into play, and the snowballing dynamic never developed, because the costs of investigation were too large to recover and because merchants of all types—those who had accidentally deceived consumers as well as the deliberate swindlers—adopted self-righteous attitudes and adamantly refused to make refunds unless subjected to the most severe pressures. That is, even before the advent of the Consumer Protection Law and the Law Enforcement Division, the Department's inspectors had been able to obtain "adjustments" for most complaining consumers by telephoning the merchants; the problem was that these adjustments rarely recognized all the rights to which the consumers were entitled.

The person who had signed up for correspondence lessons in creative writing because of a false promise that he would be able to sell short stories might get an allowance deducted from his balance, rather than a refund of the money he had already paid. Under the new law, we should have been able to secure the refund by going to court on behalf of all consumers similarly cheated, and to recover the value of the time it took us to do so, both for the Department and its cooperating complainants. The fact that we *could* obtain that recovery in court should theoretically have induced merchants to settle by making the refunds, saving themselves both the cost of defending and our cost of prosecuting. In turn, this strong incentive to settle should have kept us out of court except in rare instances, so that our modest legal staff would have been sufficient to handle the exceptional cases where litigation could not be avoided.

But merchants were never cowed by the threat of litigation; perhaps they knew that the cases would never end, and that if they did, the courts would rarely make them bear our costs as well as their own. They were far more willing to go to court than to make refunds, and since so many were willing to litigate slowly rather than settle on our terms, we quickly reached the limits of our capacity to open new investigations. When we did settle, we never recovered the full costs of our investigations; Foolproof, for example, paid $2,500 for work that had cost us at least $9,000 in Departmental time. And we never recovered a penny to compensate consumers for their time. The work of the Division, designed to be financed by involuntary contributions from those who committed consumer fraud, was actually paid for by the taxpayers. As a result, the ability of its lawyers to spread their net over all consumer fraud in the city was limited by fiscal considerations.

The government, then, cannot alone be expected to stop consumer fraud, at least not unless the courts treat consumer fraud as a serious offense or the public spends money far in excess of its present appropriations. I do not recommend the latter course in cities or states that already devote substantial legal resources to fighting consumer deception. Government has a role to play; what it can do well is to prosecute the most serious frauds. But in every urban area in which merchants and customers do not know each other by name, there will be thousands of disputes each year which cannot be settled amicably between the parties, but for which government intervention would not be economically justifiable. We can take any of several approaches toward these disputes, alone or in combination. We can ignore them, warn the public to avoid them, increase the pressure on business to prevent them, restructure the market to reduce them, or facilitate citizen initiative to remedy them in new kinds of suits and out-of-court proceedings.

To ignore the injustice that occurs when a consumer's grievance is not redressed is not totally absurd. It is to say that for all solutions to the problem, the costs of prevention or dispute settlement exceed the costs of living with the injustice. It is to recognize a certain amount of consumer fraud as one of many necessary by-products of the urban system, like dirty air or unpleasant noise, and to admit that the costs of distributing the occasional losses from the victims to a larger public, such as all buyers, or all buyers of certain types of merchandise, or the taxpayers, are not worth whatever intangible justice is thereby gained. That is, one out of every thousand buyers of wristwatches may get a lemon that the seller is unwilling to fix at his expense. As sorry as we may feel for the buyer, it may be preferable for him to suffer his loss quietly than for us to raise the prices of all wristwatches by requiring the manufacturers to adopt inspection systems that will cause only one out of a hundred thousand defective wristwatches to reach the market. Nevertheless, the cost of at least some solutions seems low compared to the cost of enduring present levels of consumer fraud. I, for one, am not now prepared to tolerate deception without attempting some further response.

Warning the public in the hope of avoiding exploitation is a proposal that, under the name of consumer education, has had a considerable following during the last decade, but seems to me of limited value. It is often suggested that a sufficient number of leaflets and radio spot announcements by government and private groups can increase the sophistication of shoppers, so that they will read advertising more skeptically, refuse the entreaties of door-to-door salesmen, read and understand contracts before signing them, and effectively refuse to accept merchandise that does not conform to advertised offers.

It seems unlikely, however, that generalized sloganeering, even if effectively communicated to the entire public, is applied by buyers to the particular circumstances of a seemingly attractive bargain. Perhaps, like health warnings on cigarette packages, deterrent slogans should be transmitted at the point of sale itself: "WARNING: The law requires us to remind you that the item in this box may not conform to the advertiser's description or the salesman's promises; if so, it is unlikely that the government or courts will help you." Such a warning, however, is likely to have even less effect than that on cigarette labels, since consumer fraud causes frustration, but rarely leads to death. Furthermore, although increased skepticism among the buying public might reduce the number of misunderstandings, many frauds can only be discovered long after the sale has been completed, when the consumer fails to receive his wig, discovers his lifetime discount privileges are worthless, or realizes he isn't interested in the magazines to which he has bought long-term subscriptions.

Warnings about particular companies might be more effective than warnings about fraud generally. The government or consumer groups might sponsor blacklists of companies that generate substantial numbers of complaints, or might systematically publicize information about those companies' activities. The Department once experimented with that type of publicity, with dramatic results, when a company had gypped dozens of unskilled laborers out of their life savings.

This company had promised the men that they would

earn $1,200 per month selling shares in Kansas oil ventures to people living in foreign countries. It had persuaded them to withdraw their savings and turn over to the company a $3,000 "bond," ostensibly to insure that once abroad "at the company's expense," the prospective salesmen did not vacation instead of work. The bonds, they were told, would be refunded when the salesmen had made a certain number of sales. The victims of this fraud were given one-way tickets to European cities, and told to go to particular hotels to attend training sessions and pick up sales kits and lists of prospects; they were also told that hotel reservations had been made for them. When they arrived, there were no training sessions, no sales kits, no prospects, and no reservations; they were stranded abroad, unable to maintain themselves, and equally unable to return to file a complaint. A few did manage to straggle back, however, and our investigation revealed that the company was still sending people abroad. The usual delay involved in using the courts was out of the question and, among other problems, most of the witnesses were out of the country and could not be brought back before the court to testify. We could not even locate them to get affidavits.

After assuring ourselves that the complaints were truthfully describing their experiences, we hired a room at the New York City Bar Association on a Saturday morning, and there convened an "investigatory hearing," with the press invited. Henry Stern played the role of hearing officer; my staff and I presented the victims who had made it back. The company was notified and invited to come and cross-examine; it chose not to. Stern made no findings at the time, nor were they necessary. The witnesses were featured on the evening television news, and stories appeared in the major newspapers, including a picture story on page four of the *Sunday Daily News*. A few days later, the company stopped doing business, and although this technique did not produce refunds, it stopped the fraud almost instantly.

While this type of specific consumer education may be effective, it does not add significantly to the number of companies whose fraud may be prevented, for its use must be extremely limited. As a practical matter, it is limited by the fact that consumers cannot remember too lengthy a blacklist for very long. And as an ethical matter, if the government or an organized group is to use its access to the media in this way at all, it must conduct a fairly thorough investigation before releasing publicity; few errors can be tolerated. Investigations are expensive, and in most cases, require obtaining information from the company, which can consume months.

A third option, likely to be experimented with increasingly as "corporate responsibility" becomes a popular concept, is to force business to police itself better, not through the self-governing trade association guidelines that have rarely worked, but through increased vulnerability for those who permit the law to be broken. This could be accomplished by increasing the penalties for consumer fraud which would be imposed not merely on the companies themselves, but on the individual executives of the companies, and on related companies. At present, the standard penalty administered to a company is an order to improve its practices in the future, hardly a deterrent to commiting fraud in the first place. The Consumer Protection Law and a Federal Trade Commission Act amendment recently passed by the United States Senate envisage mass restitution suits which would be financially painful to companies, but no such suits have yet reached the trial stage, and, as we have seen, the number of such cases that any given agency can conduct at one time is severely limited. By the time the cases are tried, the companies may disappear; in the fall of 1971, when the Department sued Enchanting Wigs for fraud and attached its assets, the balance in the company's bank account had diminished to three dollars.

Penalizing individual executives may reduce their ability to escape injury by spinning ever more corporate cocoons. When the country first started worrying about consumer fraud, in the 1910's, the states passed statutes making false advertising a crime. Later, this penalty was thought to be too

harsh, and to be an inappropriate remedy for commercial activity; the prosecutors declined to prosecute, and the injunction rather than the jail term became the standard anti-fraud
weapon. I had hoped that the indictment of Sam Stone
would signal a return to the use of the criminal law to hold
individuals accountable for the harm their corporations
cause. But the District Attorney has recently dismissed the
charges, claiming that it would be too hard to persuade a
court that Stone knew what his salesmen were telling customers.

Beyond individual responsibility is the collective responsibility of independent companies that make consumer fraud
possible. When a reputable bank, advertising agency, department store, or magazine did substantial business with a company engaged in fraud, the Department was usually able to
exert pressure by hinting at unfavorable publicity, although
the related institutions were not legally liable for the activities of the company engaged in fraud. Perhaps, though, they
should be made liable, for they either know or are in a position to ask for information about a company's selling practices. Motivated by fear of formal penalties for failure to inquire, they could serve as a first line of defense, preventing
fraud by conducting thorough investigations of the companies they dealt with. Of course, they would have to raise
the prices of their products to cover the costs of the investigations, but it may be cheaper for consumers to bear the cost
this way than for them to bear the cost of redressing fraud
after it occurs, and more just to adopt this approach than to
impose the cost of fraud on the victims alone.

A fourth approach would contemplate drastic restriction
of the market itself in categories of commercial enterprises
which historically have generated a relatively large amount
of fraud. For example, door-to-door selling, furniture retail-
ing in low-income areas, and automobile and appliance repair are among those industries that for years have been notorious sources of abuse to consumers. Two kinds of licensing
may be contemplated to regulate such problem industries.

First, licenses could be required for entry into one of these fields, and licenses granted to all applicants. The purpose of this type of licensing would be to facilitate investigation and punishment of offenders; theoretically, an agency can discipline a licensee in an administrative hearing without submitting to the cumbersome rules of procedure and evidence that apply in court. But as a practical matter, policing large numbers of licensed enterprises in an industry is no easier than policing large numbers of unlicensed enterprises. First, routinely issuing hundreds of licenses, and making the most perfunctory verification of information supplied by the applicants, is an expensive and time-consuming job. Second, detecting persons who are operating without a license is extremely costly; it depends on complaint information and requires on-site inspection. Third, punishing those who defy the licensing law is nearly impossible because the courts do not consider operating without a license a serious offense. The Department recently found that it had obtained sixty-nine convictions in three years against a Staten Island parking lot owner who had no license; the courts had fined him a total of $645, or less than ten dollars per violation, which he had passed along to his customers in the form of higher rates. Meanwhile, the Department had spent thousands of dollars worth of time establishing that he was, in each instance, still doing business, and proving that fact in court. Fourth, when a complaint is received about a licensee, the agency's prosecutorial burden is reduced only slightly by the licensee's duty to disclose; its investigative staff must still discover all the pertinent facts, and then present them at a hearing before a neutral hearing officer, taking the time of two public servants rather than one. The hearing officer, if he finds that the law has been violated, can administer only a small fine, for the courts, guardians of the right to earn a living against threats by over-zealous bureaucrats, will not uphold a severe penalty, such as license suspension, unless the offender has been proved to be a serious public enemy. Fifth, even when suspension or revocation is appropriate, appeals enable the guilty party to continue in business for years after the agency has acted. Finally, the public wrongly interprets a license as a certification of honesty even when government is impotent to enforce honesty among licensees.

Another type of licensing, in which permission to engage in the occupation is granted to only a few persons in a large geographical area, makes policing easier, because there are fewer licensees to watch, but it too has its costs. There is some genuine convenience in having an automobile repair shop, for example, in every neighborhood. If only five such shops were permitted in a city, it would be easy for an agency to watch all of them, and to keep accurate records of complaints and violations, but many consumers would be inconvenienced. Restrictive entry also gives licenses an inflated value, creating the conditions under which graft can flourish. And it promotes high prices by reducing competition. It is therefore a measure which state and local governments resort to with the greatest reluctance.

The extreme case of restrictive licensing is prohibition of an enterprise. I believe that the frequency of fraud in door-to-door credit sales not initiated by the customer suggests that this type of business, at least, if not all door-to-door selling should be abolished altogether. Its utility is slight; although there are some Americans who rarely leave their homes, most door-to-door selling is forced upon people who are quite capable of shopping for their genuine needs, in stores, in mail-order catalogs or at least by telephoning a salesman. Door-to-door sellers frequently use high-pressure techniques so that the homeowners will sign contracts just to get rid of them. They sell merchandise that few people think they want, such as encyclopedias, off-brand appliances, and correspondence lessons. They have no fixed office, and frequently change employers, so they are hard to track down and hold accountable. And by requiring consumers to sign contracts rather than pay cash, credit sellers jeopardize their customers' future earnings as well as whatever cash in the house can be used as a "small down payment." Owners of door-to-door businesses freely admitted to us that they could not effectively compel their salesmen to obey company policy; they requested that we notify them that particular salesmen were violating the law, so that they could discipline them. It is inefficient, to say the least, for government to serve as personnel manager for companies committing fraud; it is far more sensible, if a relatively useless industry cannot stop itself from violating the law, to outlaw the industry.

The approach to increased consumer protection which seems to me most likely to succeed is facilitation of individual consumer redress. As we have seen, the complex court system offers advantages to those commercial professionals who use it regularly and can achieve economies of scale, but presents a forbidding front to individual consumers who have a grievance against a merchant. Two proposals now gaining increased currency in the consumer movement could alter this imbalance: consumer class actions and the creation of neighborhood arbitration tribunals.

Class actions would be useful in those cases in which a merchant had used a common scheme to defraud between twenty and twenty thousand consumers, but government was unable to react because of limited resources, inadequate legislation, disinterested personnel, or political influence. In a class action, one consumer sues the merchant not only to get a refund or a debt cancellation for himself, but also for all of the other victims, who need not be identified until an advanced stage of the case, when they can be located through a search of the merchant's sales and credit records. Because only one case per fraud need be brought, rather than one case per victim, the consumers achieve the economies of scale which the court system usually reserves for the professional creditor; the legal and investigative fees and expenses are spread among all of the beneficiaries of the case, if the consumers win, rather than being imposed repetitiously on each of them. Since a single lawyer or group of lawyers handles the lawsuit, he can perform the investigative work and legal research a single time, for all of the represented consumers.

And since identification and location of the affected consumers can be postponed until after at least a preliminary determination that the company is guilty, that relatively costly work need be done only in those cases in which it is probably worth doing; that is, where the company will probably be held liable and has the money to pay.

Class actions have the great potential advantage of mobilizing thousands of lawyers as "private attorneys-general" to enforce the consumer protection laws; they have already had that effect in inducing lawyers to supplement government enforcement of the antitrust and securities laws. Lawyers are well compensated to institute class actions on behalf of stockholders who have been cheated; if they win, the courts award them counsel fees amounting to between ten and thirty percent of recoveries amounting to tens of thousands or even millions of dollars. Of course, when so much money is at stake, the defendants fight vigorously and the cases take years; still, because the fees are set in relation to the difficulty of the cases, attorneys are willing to do the work, and supplemental law enforcement is a welcome by-product. In fact, securities lawyers generally concede that the fear of class actions, rather than fear of government prosecution, is what keeps the stock market honest. The deterrent of potential class actions is more credible than the threat of suit by the Securities and Exchange Commission because there exists only one Commission, but potentially thousands of lawyers who could start class actions. Where class actions are permitted, no violator can gamble on a government agency being swamped by time-consuming litigation against other swindlers.

At present, only a few states, such as California and Massachusetts, permit class actions on behalf of consumers. In most of the other states, legislation appears to permit such cases, but the courts have protected business by giving the statutes tortured meanings, practically prohibiting the suits. In Congress, Robert C. Eckhardt, a Texas Democrat, has conducted a three-year crusade for a federal bill to permit consumer class actions, but intensive lobbying by the so-called "legitimate" segments of industry—the national associations of department stores, automobile dealers, grocery manufacturers, canners, and others—and the opposition of President Nixon, have prevented the House Committee on Interstate and Foreign Commerce from even voting on the bill. Chief Justice Warren Burger entered the legislative battle on the side of the President in 1970, by stating in a widely reported speech that the federal courts had enough to do without having to decide consumer cases.

Despite this opposition, class actions will be an important consumer remedy within a few years. Already, in those few states which permit this type of consumer suit, they have produced significant gains for consumer justice. An Illinois consumer class action forced one of the nation's largest mail-order houses to credit the accounts of thousands of its credit customers, to which it had unlawfully added certain insurance charges. In California, an action is pending to force one of the country's automobile manufacturers to pay for replacement of defective wheels on 200,000 trucks; shortly after the case was filed, the company offered to pay for new wheels for 40,000 of the trucks for which the defective wheels were most likely to cause accidents. The California Supreme Court has also ruled valid a consumer class action to recover damages for the many victims of a food-freezer swindle similar to the one that entrapped Mr. Allen. And consumers around the country will benefit from the settlement of a treble-damages class action against the drug companies that for a period of years unlawfully fixed the prices of antibiotics. While these cases illustrate the potential utility of the class action device, it is plain that consumer class actions are in their infancy, and that the time for their further development is at hand. Perhaps a change in national administrations will spur their growth.

Class actions, however, are of no value—deterrent or redistributive—where the deception is of a type affecting each consumer differently. If a company's door-to-door salesmen are clever enough to tailor their fraudulent statements to the tastes of each sales prospect, few common threads of law and fact will exist to unite the victims, and little time or money will be saved by lawyers representing more than one of them at a time. Each case will have to be tried individually.

But to say that each consumer will have to tell his own story is not to say that he must tell it to his lawyer, to the merchant's lawyer, and then a third time to a judge. It is not to say that he must pay an expert to help him fill out complex forms or miss work to appear in a huge, intimidating courtroom across town or in a neighboring city. It is not to say that he must lose his case because he cannot find a lawyer willing to represent him. The expansion of consumer class actions—the biggest type of consumer case—must be accompanied by the creation of new institutions to handle the many grievances not susceptible to class action treatment.

If we seriously propose to give the defrauded consumer a genuine day in court, we must remove consumer cases from the low-level civil courts that serve as collection agencies in most urban areas and create entirely new forums for the smallest type of consumer case. These tribunals must be sufficiently convenient and informal for consumers to participate in their proceedings. They alone should hear consumer cases involving claims under $3,000, whether initiated by consumers or alleged creditors. Each one should serve an area no larger than a school district or a state assembly district, so that access is not a problem; they should convene in each district only often enough to keep them busy. At least half the time, they should be open during the evening, or on weekends, so that people who work need not have to choose between justice and their jobs.

They should hear evidence in an orderly but informal manner, and should dispense with those rules of procedure—such as the need to proceed by direct and cross-examination—which befuddle ordinary citizens. Participants in their deliberation should be entitled to representation by counsel if they so desire, but sufficient informality and the assistance of paraprofessional advocates on the tribunal's staff should enable citizens to appear alone without disadvantage. The "judges" need not be judges at all; they could be lawyers, law students, or community volunteers acceptable to both parties, but they should serve often enough to develop familiarity with particular companies involved in the cases and the practices in which they engage, a familiarity that would enable them to draw correct inferences from somewhat incomplete evidence that untrained consumers might present. The proceedings, then, would be more akin to neighborhood arbitration than to current court practice.

I, for one, would not be saddened to see courts give way to new institutions designed to redress consumer grievances, or to punish low-level white collar crime. The courts have had an opportunity to do the job; they have failed to do it by themselves, and they have frustrated government agencies established to stop consumer fraud. The Kerner Commission found consumer problems to be among the most intense grievances underlying the riots of 1967, and recommended "effective utilization of the courts." "Through the adversary process which is at the heart of our judicial system," the Commission said, "litigants are afforded meaningful opportunity to influence events which affect them and their community." The brave words don't ring true. The adversary process only works when there are adversaries, and only works well when the adversaries are roughly equal in the quality of their representation and the courts are sensitive to injustices that cannot always be proved by formal rules of procedure and within the confines of each case. The promotion of consumer rights will require the establishment of new types of courts, the use of new procedures, and the emergence of lawyers and judges who see litigation not as an intricate system for postponing decisions but as a way of achieving justice.